The Arts and Crafts BUSY BOOK

Trish Kuffner

Meadowbrook Press

Distributed by Simon & Schuster
New York

Library of Congress Cataloging-in-Publication Data
Kuffner, Trish.
    The arts and crafts busy book : 365 art and craft activities to keep
    toddlers and preschoolers busy / by Trish Kuffner.
        p. cm.
    Includes bibliographical references and index.
    ISBN 0-88166-434-0 (Meadowbrook) ISBN 0-684-01872-1 (Simon & Schuster)
        1. Handicraft. 2. Creative activities and seat work—Handbooks,
    manuals, etc. I. Title.
    TT157 .K84 2003
    745.5—dc21

                                                    2002152798

Editorial Director: Christine Zuchora-Walske
Editor: Megan McGinnis
Proofreader: Angela Wiechmann
Production Manager: Paul Woods
Art Director: Peggy Bates
Desktop Publishing: Danielle White
Cover Art: Dorothy Stott
Illustrations: Laurel Aiello

Published by Meadowbrook Press, 5451 Smetana Drive, Minnetonka, Minnesota 55343

www.meadowbrookpress.com

BOOK TRADE DISTRIBUTION by Simon and Schuster, a division of Simon and
Schuster, Inc., 1230 Avenue of the Americas, New York, NY 10020

08 07 06 05   10 9 8 7 6 5 4 3 2

Printed in the United States of America

Dedication

For Wayne, who has given me twenty years, five children, and more love than I deserve.

Acknowledgments

I wrote my first book a number of years ago as the frustrated mother of three very young children. Ten years later, I've written several more books and had two more children. I couldn't have done either without the help of some wonderful people.

First, as always, I acknowledge my ability to do all that I do only by the grace of God and through the wisdom, strength, and patience He gives me every day.

I have a great group of friends without whose support I couldn't be the woman, mother, and writer that I am: Joy and Karen, our walks keep me fit; Janine, our talks keep me sane; Leslie, you keep me laughing; Frances, you keep me in line; Diane, Kathy, Kimberly, and Sue, you hearten me with your friendship.

Writing this book was possible in part because of the valuable help of Lynn Grala, a young South African who came to live with our family for a time. Lynn, I couldn't have shut myself away all those days were it not for you.

Writing books while raising and home-schooling five kids means a sacrifice of one thing or another. My children forgive me when the refrigerator is empty, when I miss family outings, and when my mind is elsewhere even when I'm with them. I so love and appreciate you, Andria, Emily, Joshua, Johanna, and Samuel. You're the best part of my life.

I have journeyed these past twenty years with a loving husband whom I think I often take for granted. Wayne, I didn't know raising a family would be so difficult, tiring, frustrating, self-sacrificing, rewarding, exciting, and wonderful; did you? Thanks for putting up with me through it all.

Finally, to my U.S. publishing team at Meadowbrook Press and my Canadian distributor, Sandhill Book Marketing, thanks for your ongoing support and guidance. You continue to make writing a reality for me, and I appreciate all that you do.

Contents

Introduction vii

Chapter 1:
Arts and Crafts 1
Organizing and Planning for
  Arts and Crafts 2
Stocking Up on Supplies 5
Arts and Crafts for Toddlers . . . 9
Voilà! What Now? 11
One Last Thought 12

Chapter 2:
Scribbling, Coloring,
and Drawing 13

Chapter 3:
Painting 43

Chapter 4:
Printmaking 79

Chapter 5:
Modeling, Sculpting,
and Papier-Mâché . . . 97

Chapter 6:
Glue, Paper, and
Scissors 135

Chapter 7:
Nature Arts
and Crafts 163

Chapter 8:
Edible Arts
and Crafts 189

Chapter 9:
Educational Arts
and Crafts 225

Chapter 10:
Toys, Gifts,
and More 253

Chapter 11:
Holiday Arts
and Crafts 287
Valentine's Day 289
Saint Patrick's Day 296

Easter 304
Canada Day 313
Independence Day 318
Halloween 325
Thanksgiving 332
Hanukkah 339
Christmas 348
Kwanzaa 362

Appendixes **369**
Appendix A: Basic Craft
 Recipes 369
  Paint 369

Play Dough 374
Clay 376
Glue and Paste 378
Other Craft Recipes . . . 379
Appendix B: Making
 Books with Children 382
Appendix C: Books for
 Children 384
Appendix D: Resources
 for Parents 386

Index **389**

Introduction

When Meadowbrook Press asked me to write an arts and crafts book for parents of young children, a few eyebrows were raised around our house. It's not that I dislike arts and crafts, but I've always felt somewhat artistically challenged! I've favored simple activities, like painting or modeling with play dough, over those requiring several supplies to make elaborate objects. To me, if an arts and crafts book has glossy photos or diagrams and detailed instructions, the projects are way too complicated to do with kids!

I began writing activity books in part because I wanted projects that would keep my kids busy, that used materials found around the house, that were simple to set up and clean up, and that—most of all—required minimal adult involvement or supervision. After all, having three children under age three, I barely sat down during the day, much less spent precious time organizing a complicated activity.

Things haven't changed much over the past ten years. In addition to having two more children and writing books, home-schooling keeps me busy, so I don't have any more free time than I did when I wrote my first book. While the kinds of activities we do together have changed as my children have grown, I still have the same requirements for most projects we undertake. They must use fairly basic materials, must ideally be process-oriented (focus on the creative process, not the product), and must be simple enough for the kids to do without my constant assistance or supervision. You'll find such arts and crafts activities in this book.

Some ideas in *The Art and Crafts Busy Book* appear in other books I've written, and I've included them to provide the best arts and crafts activities for young children. I've organized the activities by category, but many of them can fit into two or more categories. For example, papier-mâché crafts make excellent gifts, and seasonal materials turn educational arts and crafts into holiday projects.

Children's abilities between the ages of two and six vary greatly, so some ideas in this book will be too advanced for a two-year-old, while others will be too simple for a six-year-old. Because a child's development often isn't related to his age, I don't suggest age ranges for the activities. Choose activities that best meet your child's capabilities and interests. If a new activity doesn't go over well, don't write it off altogether. Try it again later, or vary the activity to make it more meaningful and interesting for your child.

Have fun crafting with your child. If you have any questions or comments about *The Arts and Crafts Busy Book*, you can e-mail me or write to me in care of Meadowbrook Press. I'd love to hear from you.

Trish

P.S. In recognition of the fact that children do indeed come in both sexes, and in an effort to represent each, the use of masculine and feminine pronouns will alternate with each chapter.

CHAPTER 1
Arts and Crafts

Creativity is allowing yourself to make mistakes. Art is knowing which ones to keep.

—*Scott Adams*

Most young children have an abundance of three things: energy, curiosity, and creativity. That's why so many of them love arts and crafts. Experimenting with paint, glue, play dough, scissors, paper, and markers focuses their energy constructively, helps them learn about the world around them, and allows them to explore and express their creativity. Whether at home, daycare, preschool, church, or playgroup, many young children take part in arts and crafts every day with their parents, caregivers, or teachers.

Some adults may enjoy arts and crafts because they understand how important it is for young children to express themselves creatively, or they may simply enjoy doing arts and crafts. Yet many adults shudder when they hear the words *arts and crafts*. They think of messy, complicated projects that require expensive supplies and a lot of time. They may not enjoy doing arts and crafts and may dislike having to correct children's mistakes or finish their projects.

While arts and crafts projects *can* be expensive, messy, complicated, and time-consuming, they need *not* be so.

Projects that use basic supplies, that are simple and quick, and that let the child explore and create with minimal supervision and intervention can be rewarding for both adults and children. Such projects succeed because they emphasize the creative process and not the product being created.

While most of the activities in this book are open-ended and process oriented, some activities do focus on creating a certain product, like a moss wreath, beaded coaster, or shamrock shape. Your child will benefit from doing these projects if you don't emphasize how you think the product should look. Don't try to finish the project "the right way." Let your child decide when and how to finish her work.

ORGANIZING AND PLANNING FOR ARTS AND CRAFTS

Organize your supplies and plan activities so children have easy access to materials and have a wide variety of experiences each day. Here are a few points to keep in mind:

Provide an environment that's conducive to creativity. It's hard to be creative when kids (or their parents) worry about getting marker on the table, paint on the walls, or play dough in the carpet.

- Provide a small table and chair for your child to use.
- Work in an uncarpeted area, where spills can easily be wiped up. If you like, cover the floor and/or tabletop with an old sheet or plastic tablecloth.
- Keep clean up supplies like sponges and old towels nearby so your child can help clean up.
- Use art smocks or old T-shirts to protect clothing.

Have arts and crafts supplies organized and accessible.
Organize and store supplies in a cupboard or bookcase. Be safety conscious. Keep any dangerous items well out of reach.

- Use clear plastic bins for storage. Sort supplies and label each bin (crayons, markers, clay, play dough, and so on).
- Spice containers or a tackle box is great for storing small items like googly eyes, beads, buttons, and so on.
- Store paper in stackable desk trays.
- Use a lazy Susan or a shower caddy to hold glue bottles, tape dispensers, paint jars, and so on.
- An open box or basket will hold large items like egg cartons, toilet paper tubes, coffee cans, used greeting cards, pine cones, Styrofoam trays, and other wonderful craft supplies.

Choose age-appropriate materials and activities.
Provide materials and activities that are appropriate for your child's age and development.

- Generally, toddlers best use crayons, play dough, chalk, and paint. Young preschoolers enjoy finger and easel painting, printmaking, making collages, and sculpting with moldable materials like clay. Older preschoolers have better small motor skills and can use scissors, smaller paintbrushes, and colored pencils, as well as do activities like beading, sewing, and so on.

- Remember that a child's age doesn't always indicate her development, so don't choose activities based on what you think a two-year-old should be doing or on what your neighbor's two-year-old is doing. I don't suggest age ranges for the activities in this book so you can choose activities based on your child's abilities and interests.

- Choose activities that are challenging, but not so difficult that your child will become frustrated.

- A young child learns by using her senses. When possible, choose activities that use all your child's senses.

- When possible, choose activities your child can work on and complete by herself. (My philosophy is if a project needs photos, diagrams, and lengthy instructions, it's surely too complicated for a young child to do. You won't find any such activities in this book.)

- Consider your own needs, interests, skills, and abilities when planning activities for your child. A good attitude is crucial for the success of any activity you choose.

Plan arts and crafts activities ahead of time.

Here are guidelines to help you plan activities for your child:

- Browse this book and make a list of the activities you'd like your child to do alone, with you, or with your family.
- Create a weekly plan from your list of activities. Be realistic—you may not be able to do something every day.
- Make a list of anything you'll need to do ahead of time, such as buy paint, make a batch of modeling clay, and so on.
- Plan special activities for your baby sitter to do with your child, and have all the necessary materials handy.
- Make a list of fun activities to do anytime you can fit them into your schedule. Have this list ready for a rainy day, sick day, or when you have some free time.

STOCKING UP ON SUPPLIES

The activities in this book require basic supplies. You can easily find many of the following items around the home.

alphabet cereal or
  pasta
aluminum foil
aluminum pie pan
art smock or old
  T-shirt
balloons
balls (tennis, golf,
  Koosh)

beads (assorted)
beeswax sheets
bingo dabbers
birdseed
bottle (empty roll-
  on deodorant or
  shoe polish)
bottle caps
boxes

broom
bubble wrap
burlap
buttons
calculator paper
calendars (old and
  current)
camera
candles

candlewick
candy or soap mold
canning jars
cardboard
catalogs
cellophane
ceramic tile
   (assorted)
cereal boxes
chalk
chicken wire
chopsticks
clay
clear acrylic spray
clear contact paper
clear nail polish
clothespins
coffee cans (with
   lids)
coffee filters
coins
cold-water dye
colored pencils
comb (rubber or
   metal)
compact disc cases
   (empty)

cookie cutters
corks
corncob holders
cotton balls
cotton swabs
craft foam
craft wire
crayons (whole
   and broken)
crepe paper
darning needle
decoupage glue
dishwand
drinking straws
dry beans
dry pasta
   (assorted)
duct tape
egg cartons
elastic cord
envelopes
Epsom salts
erasers (regular
   and art gum)
eyedropper
fabric crayons
fabric dye

fabric scraps
feathers
felt
film canisters
   (empty)
florist's foam
fly swatter
food coloring
funnel
gel pens
gift-wrap scraps
glitter
glitter glue
glue
glue gun
glue sticks
googly eyes
grass seeds
greeting cards
   (used)
grocery store fliers
hair gel
hole punch
ice cream buckets
   (empty)
index cards
jars and lids

jellybeans
juice cans
knitting needles
liquid bleach
liquid dish soap
liquid starch
magazines (old)
magnetic strips
magnets
marbles
markers (permanent and washable)
matte board
medicine and pill bottles with lids
metal jar or juice can lids
modeling compound
nail polish
necktie (old)
newspapers
newsprint
notebooks
note cards

paint (acrylic, fabric, tempera)
paint swatches
paint pens
paint stick
"paint with water" book
paintbrushes
paint rollers
pantyhose
paper (construction and plain)
paper bags
paper clips
paper doilies
paper fasteners
paper lunch bags
paper plates
paper scraps
paper towels
paper towel and toilet paper tubes
pencils
pens
petroleum jelly
phone books (old)

photo album (small)
photos of friends and family
pine cones
pinking shears
pipe cleaners
plaster of Paris
plastic berry baskets
plastic dishpan
plastic mesh
plastic page protectors
plastic tablecloth
plastic wrap
Popsicle mold
Popsicle sticks
poster board
poster putty
potpourri
printing ink
pumpkinseeds
pushpins
ribbon
rice
rickrack

rolling pin
rubber bands
rubber cement
rubber stamps
ruler
salad spinner
sand
sandpaper
scissors
scouring pads
scrapbook
sequins
sewing needles
shellac
shells
shallow box
shaving cream
shoe polish (black)
shoeboxes with lids
shoelaces
soap, bar (Ivory)
soap, clear liquid
soap flakes
soap powder
soda can
socks (old and new)
Spanish moss

sponges
spice containers
  (empty)
spray bottle
squeeze bottles
stamp pad
stapler
stickers (assorted)
stones
straight pins
string
Styrofoam balls
  and blocks
Styrofoam cups
  and trays
Styrofoam wreath
  (heart- or circle-
  shaped)
sugar cubes
tape (transparent,
  masking, col-
  ored)
tape measure
terra cotta pots
three-ring binders
thumbtacks
tin cans (empty)

tissue paper
thread
thread spools
  (empty)
toilet paper
toothbrushes (old)
toothpicks
towel (old)
twist-ties
utility knife
Velcro
wallpaper books
walnut shells
wax paper
wine bottle (empty)
wire clothes
  hanger
wood blocks
wood scraps
wooden dowels
wooden spoon
writing pads
yarn scraps
Ziploc bags
zippers (6- or 7-
  inch length)

ARTS AND CRAFTS FOR TODDLERS

Your toddler benefits from an arts and crafts activity when you let her smell the finger paint, feel it with her hands, see how one color changes when another is added, and so on. So focus on the sensory experience of the activity. (Remember: It's the process that counts, not the product.)

Arts and crafts activities won't benefit your toddler if you do most of the work. We all know arts and crafts look better, go faster, and are neater if we do the work, but if toddlers are to learn from an activity, they have to do the work themselves. Any skills your toddler may have learned will be lost or minimized if you do the activity for her. Even something as simple as using a glue stick is important for little ones, so don't grab it out of your child's hands and do it yourself if she's not using it "right."

Karen Miller, in her book *More Things to Do with Toddlers and Twos* (Telshare Publishing Company Ltd., 1990), lists general principles for doing art projects with toddlers. Although she writes primarily for teachers of toddlers, her guidelines are great to keep in mind when working on arts and crafts projects with one or many toddlers.

- Don't tell your toddler what to make, and don't expect her artwork to be recognizable. Expecting a two-year-old to make a mailbox or an Easter basket only sets her up for failure. Instead, Miller says, "value the basic scribble."

Toddlers simply don't have the motor control necessary to make representational artwork. Just let your toddler freely explore materials and techniques.

- Provide various materials. Toddlers are interested in cause and effect, whether they're playing with water, building with blocks, or finger painting, pasting, or painting with a brush. Expose her to as many different materials as possible. Let her play with warm play dough one day, cold the next. Mix paint thick one time, thin another. Paint with wide and narrow paintbrushes, sponges, and feathers.

- Let your toddler do the whole project. For her, the value of making a collage with glue comes from spreading the glue, noticing how it feels on her fingers, and so on.

- Do projects with one toddler or with very small groups. Older toddlers may enjoy doing projects in groups of three or four. If you care for several children, have other things for them to do while you're working one-on-one with your toddler, or allow them to watch.

- Allow children to repeat experiences. Sometimes we think providing a variety of experiences for our children means never doing the same thing twice. But allowing your child to repeat an activity lets her fully explore it and, as Miller states, "encourages the development of concentration and experimentation, both elements of creativity."

VOILÀ! WHAT NOW?

Children who love to do arts and crafts create lots of stuff, often leaving parents wondering what to do with it. Some kids don't care if their creations are saved, and some need to know it's okay to throw away something just made. (If you've focused on the creative process, then the product won't be so important.) But most kids and adults like to admire their art-work before it's tossed out. Here are a few suggestions:

- Display your child's artwork whenever and wherever you can. Post it on walls, doors, and the refrigerator. Cover your table with a solid dark tablecloth, arrange your child's artwork on it, then cover it with a clear tablecloth. Visit a frame shop and ask to have mat scraps saved for you. Use them to mount or frame your child's artwork.
- Give your child's artwork away. Many of the projects in this book create lovely gifts, gift-wrap, cards, and so on. Or create unique calendars by collecting free calendars from local businesses and gluing your child's artwork into them.
- Save your child's best artwork in a portfolio. A portfolio catalogs your child's artistic development. Use a three-ring binder with plastic page protectors, and date or write your child's age on the artwork. Have your child help choose what to include in her portfolio. For extralarge or three-dimensional projects, take photos of them and put them in the binder.

- Discreetly throw away what you can't save. Your child won't miss a picture or two, but seeing her artwork in the wastebasket may cause heartache for you both.

ONE LAST THOUGHT

Well-planned arts and crafts activities help your child feel good about herself and her abilities. Children become more creative when they can go at their own pace and figure out their own ways of doing things. Have reasonable expectations, and concentrate on the creative process, not the product.

Remember that arts and crafts projects are forms of self-expression, and your child should know there is no right or wrong way to create art. With the right attitude, and a little planning and organizing, you and your child will have a wonderful time creating, exploring, and discovering the world of arts and crafts.

CHAPTER 2
Scribbling, Coloring, and Drawing

Every child is an artist. The problem is how to remain an artist once he grows up.

—Pablo Picasso

Drawing is probably the first art form your child will experience. It's simple and fun, and it can be done anywhere and anytime. It's something most of us do, in some form or another, all our lives.

Scribbling is usually a toddler's first attempt at drawing. At first he may do little more than chew the crayon and crumple the paper. But most toddlers soon find scribbling a lot of fun. It allows them to experiment with cause and effect while developing small motor skills and hand-eye coordination. Cynthia Catlin, in her book *Toddlers Together: The Complete Planning Guide for a Toddler Curriculum* (Gryphon House, 1994), says, "Scribbling is the precursor to writing, just as babbling is to talking."

Preschoolers continue to experiment with cause and effect and use their developing small motor skills and hand-eye coordination to produce recognizable drawings. While they enjoy using the same materials over and over, they also appreciate drawing with various tools and on various surfaces.

As children enter middle childhood, they begin to create more realistic-looking drawings, although they may get easily frustrated when their efforts don't yield the desired results. Your child may enjoy drawing lessons from an art class or a book. We've used *Drawing with Children* by Mona Brookes (J. P. Tarcher, 1996), and the Draw Write Now series by Marie Hablitzel and Kim Stitzer (Barker Creek Publishing, Inc.).

The following ideas will help encourage your child's drawing efforts:

- Give your child a variety of drawing tools, including crayons, pens, pencils, colored pencils, chalk, markers, and charcoal.
- Give your child a variety of papers, including plain paper, construction paper, newsprint, tracing paper, shiny paper, fine sandpaper, cardboard, and matte board.
- Cut paper into shapes like circles, triangles, and stars.
- Give your child three-dimensional surfaces like boxes and rocks to draw on.
- Give your child a notebook or sketchbook to draw in.
- Let your child draw while you read a book to him.
- Encourage your child to draw pictures in various shades of the same color.

Encourage your child to experiment and express himself through drawing. Make sure he understands that while certain techniques will yield more realistic-looking results, there's no right or wrong way to draw.

Crazy Crayons

Use these ideas to make use of broken crayon pieces.

*Broken crayon pieces,
  paper removed
Clean, empty tin cans
Pot of very hot water
Plastic film canisters*

*Candy or soap mold
  (optional)
Muffin pan
Aluminum foil (optional)*

- Have your child sort the crayon pieces by color. Place the pieces in the tin cans, one color per can. Set the tin cans in a pot of very hot water until the crayons have melted. Pour a small amount (approximately ¼ inch) into each film canister. When the wax hardens, add a second color in the same way. Continue this process until you have a crayon that's a rainbow of layered colors. Or if you like, pour the melted wax into a candy or soap mold to make a shaped crayon.
- Preheat your oven to 400°F. Have your child place the crayon pieces in a well-greased muffin pan (or a muffin pan lined with aluminum foil), one color per section. Or to make the crayons have a stained glass effect, mix the colors. Place the pan in the oven for a few minutes, until the crayons have melted. Remove the pan from the oven and let the crayons cool completely before removing them from the pan.

Easel Art

If crayon marks on the wall are a problem in your home, try the following ideas to rein in your runaway artist.

Tape
Large sheet of drawing
  paper
Art easel
Fat crayons
Yarn
Scissors

Large cardboard box
Hammer and nails

- Tape the paper to the easel. Cut several 2-foot lengths of yarn. Cut a small notch at one end of each crayon and wrap and tie a length of yarn around it. Tie the other end of the yarn to the top of the easel. (Be sure to cut the yarn long enough to reach the paper, but not so long that it poses a choking hazard.)
- Make a tabletop easel by removing the top and bottom flaps and one side panel of a cardboard box and taping the remaining three side panels together to form a triangle. Tape the bottom of the easel to the table and attach paper to one side. If you like, attach crayons with yarn as specified above.
- Turn a blank wall in the basement or playroom into a drawing center. Tape the paper to the wall. Above the paper, hammer in a few nails and attach the yarn and crayons to the nails.

Crayon Basics

Encourage your child to explore the versatility of his crayons.

Crayons
Variety of paper (plain, colored, construction, wax, shiny,
  newsprint, and so on)

- Use the pointed end of the crayon to make thin lines, and the blunt end or the side of the crayon to make thick lines.
- Press firmly for solid, heavy colors. Press lightly for more subtle hues.
- Experiment with making clusters of dots, lines, swirls, and so on.

Use a variety of paper and observe the effect when each is colored with crayons.

Marker Play

Most children would rather draw with markers than with anything else. Here are a few suggestions to help your child get the most out of his markers.

Markers (permanent and washable)
Water
Paper towel or coffee filter
Paper
Paintbrush or sponge
Plaster of Paris
Small plastic container

- Show your child how to dip dried-up markers in water and paint with them like watercolors. When the tips turn white, throw them away or use them as paintbrushes.
- Let your child draw with a thick black marker on a paper towel or coffee filter. Brush water over the picture with a paintbrush or sponge, then watch the color seep.
- Brush paper with water using a paintbrush or sponge. Let your child draw with washable markers on the wet paper and watch the colors run and blend.

Make a marker holder by mixing plaster of Paris in a small plastic container that's at least as deep as a marker cap. Set the caps in the wet plaster with the open ends up. Keep the plaster clear of the open ends. When the plaster is dry, press the markers into their tops.

Drawing Challenge

Paper
Crayons, colored pencils, or markers
Mirror
Blindfold
Clothespin
Tape

- Challenge your child to draw a simple picture or write his name with his non-dominant hand.
- Challenge your child to write a message or his name backward and hold it up to a mirror to see how he did.
- Have your child close his eyes and try to draw a simple picture or write his name or a message.
- Blindfold your child or have him close his eyes, then have him draw randomly. Remove the blindfold and take turns looking for hidden shapes or objects in the drawing.
- Clip a clothespin onto a crayon and challenge your child to draw by holding the clothespin.
- Tape two or more crayons together and let your child draw a picture with them.

Poster Child

Very large sheet of newsprint or other paper
Markers, crayons, or colored pencils
Stapler and newspaper (optional)

Have your child lie on the paper on the floor. Trace around his body, then have him stand to see the outline you've drawn. For a toddler, help him draw features with markers, crayons, or colored pencils. A preschooler will be able to add the features himself. Have him be as detailed as possible: What is his hair like? What color are his eyes? What clothes is he wearing? When he's finished, hang the poster somewhere he can admire it.

If you like, make a three-dimensional tracing. Stack two sheets of paper on the floor and have your child lie on the paper. Trace around his body, drawing about an inch or two away from his body. Cut out the tracings and staple them together at the sides, leaving the top and bottom open. Have your child decorate both sides as specified above. Stuff the shape with crumpled newspaper, then staple the top and bottom closed.

Body Tracing

Drawing paper
Crayons, colored pencils, or markers
Nail polish, glitter glue, or paint (optional)

- Have your child stand on the paper while you trace around his feet. Use another sheet of paper and have him trace your feet. Compare sizes.
- Place your child's hands on the paper and trace around them. Have him do the same for you, then compare the tracings.
- Color in the traced hands and feet. If you like, use nail polish, glitter glue, or paint to add rings and polish to the fingers and toes.

My Day Poster

Markers, crayons, or colored pencils
Writing paper or poster board
Stapler and construction paper
Crayons, markers, or stickers

Talk with your child about what he normally does every day:
wake up, eat breakfast, play outside, read, watch TV, and so
on. Make a list, poster, or book using words or pictures to
describe the activities you've discussed. If you're making a
book, staple sheets of paper together inside a construction
paper cover or follow the directions in Appendix B, then
write one activity on each page. Let your child decorate the
list, poster, or book with crayons, markers, or stickers.

Silhouette Portrait

Desk lamp
Table
Tape
Large sheet of paper
Markers, crayons, or colored pencils

Place a desk lamp on a table about 6 feet from a blank wall.
Have your child stand against the wall so his profile casts a
shadow on the wall behind him. Tape the paper to the wall,
in the shadow, and trace your child's silhouette. When the
tracing is complete, let your child use markers, crayons, or
colored pencils to add details to the portrait.

Budding Illustrator

Making a book with your child is a fun way to encourage a child who likes to write or illustrate stories. A book can be:

- paper stapled together inside a construction paper cover
- a small notebook with blank pages
- an inexpensive scrapbook
- a three-ring binder with plastic page protectors
- a hand-bound volume (See Appendix B.)

Let your child write a story (or dictate a story for you to write) along the bottom of each page and illustrate it with crayons, colored pencils, or markers.

I rode into the forest

and saw a spotted dragon!

Eraser Art

This activity is easy and fun for toddlers. Preschoolers may enjoy using the eraser as a drawing tool and rubbing off the color in a pattern or design.

Tape
Large sheet of paper
Colored pencils or pastels
Large eraser (preferably an art gum eraser)

Tape the paper to a low table or your toddler's highchair tray. Scribble, or have your child scribble, all over the paper with colored pencils or pastels. Give your child a large eraser and show him how to rub off the color in a design.

Dots and Lines

Colorful dot stickers
Paper
Crayons or washable markers

Give your child the stickers. Let him stick the dots onto his paper at random. Older children will enjoy using a crayon or marker to connect the dots.

Chalk Fun

Your child can use store-bought or homemade chalk (see Appendix A) in many different, creative ways.

Colored chalk
Paper
Hair spray
Sponge or paintbrush
Water, liquid starch, or buttermilk
⅓ cup sugar
Cotton ball

- Have your child draw with chalk on paper. Spray the drawing with hair spray to set the chalk.
- Use a sponge or paintbrush to paint paper with water, liquid starch, or buttermilk. While it's still wet, have your child make designs on the paper with chalk.
- Place paper on a textured surface (like a sidewalk) or over a greeting card with a raised design. Have your child rub chalk over the paper to make a chalk rubbing of the texture or design.
- Soak chalk in a mixture of 1 cup water and ⅓ cup sugar for 5–10 minutes. Let your child draw on paper with the wet chalk, then smudge the drawing with a cotton ball.
- Let your child draw on a window with wet chalk. (It will easily wash away.)

Paint Pens

Although called paint pens, these are actually more of a drawing tool than a painting tool. They are available at craft stores in plain, glitter, and scented colors. The paint stays raised when dry and gives artwork a three-dimensional effect.

Pencil
Plain or construction paper
Paint pens

Thick black marker
Matte board (optional)
Crayon, paper removed

- Have your child use a pencil to draw a picture or design on the paper. Help him trace over the lines with the paint pens.
- On the paper, use the marker to draw a long, twisting line that crosses itself many times. Have your child fill in the spaces with the paint pens, varying the color and design from space to space. If you like, mount the drawing on paper or matte board and hang it to display.
- Use a paint pen to make birthday invitations and thank-you cards. Write the words *You're Invited* or *Thank You* with a paint pen on the paper. When the paint has dried, fold sheets of paper into halves or quarters to make cards, then lay the front of each card faceup on the raised words. Show your child how to rub the side of a crayon over the words to transfer the message to the card.

Wax Resist Rubbings

Paper
Corrugated cardboard or other textured surface
Crayon, paper removed
Paintbrush
Paint
Black crayon or permanent marker

Lay the paper on the cardboard. Show your child how to rub the side of a crayon over the paper so the pattern of the textured surface appears on the paper. Brush paint in a contrasting color over the wax rubbing. When the paint is dry, display the rubbing as is, have your child draw a picture on it with a black crayon or permanent marker, or use it as the background for another art project.

Texture Rubbings

Textured objects like leaves, string, doilies, paper clips, keys, fabric, tiles, coins, and bricks
Scissors and cardboard (optional)
Paper
Tape (optional)
Crayons, paper removed

Gather a collection of textured objects. If you like, cut shapes from cardboard. Place paper over a textured object or cardboard shape. If you like, tape the corners of the paper to the work surface to prevent the paper from moving. Show your child how to rub the side of the crayon on the paper over the object. Shift the paper and change colors for an interesting effect.

Crayon Design

Because this activity requires a food warming tray or electric griddle, it's recommended for older preschoolers who are closely supervised by an adult.

Paper or aluminum foil
Food warming tray or electric griddle
Oven mitt or thick glove
Crayons
Black marker (optional)

Place the paper or foil on a food warming tray or electric griddle set on low. Cover your child's non-dominant hand with an oven mitt or thick glove and tell him to hold the paper still with that hand. With his drawing hand, have your child rub a crayon slowly on the warm paper to make a melted crayon design. Remind your child to keep his bare skin off the warming tray or griddle.

If you like, have your child use a black marker to outline a design on the paper. Place the paper on the warming tray or griddle and have him use crayons to color in the design to create a stained glass effect.

Melted-Crayon Drawing

Because this activity requires a food warming tray or electric griddle, it's recommended for older preschoolers who are closely supervised by an adult.

Food warming tray or electric griddle
Aluminum foil
Crayons, paper removed
Cotton swabs
Construction paper

Cover a food warming tray or electric griddle with aluminum foil, and set the appliance on low. Place several crayons in various colors on the aluminum foil. Leave space between the crayons so the colors won't run together.

When the wax has melted, have your child dip a cotton swab into the melted wax and paint a design on construction paper. Remind your child to keep his bare skin off the warming tray or griddle.

Paper Batik

Construction paper
Crayons
Liquid tempera paint in a dark color
Paintbrush
Newspaper
Hot iron

Have your child completely color the paper with crayons. He can draw an abstract design, or draw an object in the foreground and color in the background with a contrasting color. When the drawing is complete, show him how to crumple the paper carefully into a tight ball, then gently unfold the picture and notice how the surface has cracked. Brush dark-colored paint on the paper to create a mosaic effect. Rinse the picture under a tap and allow it to dry. When the picture is dry, place it between two sheets of newspaper and gently iron it to smooth the wrinkles.

Fabric Transfers

Fabric crayons
Paper
T-shirt, book bag, pillowcase, or other fabric item
Iron

Have your child use fabric crayons to draw a picture or design on the paper. Place the paper crayon side down on the T-shirt or other fabric item, and iron it to transfer the picture to the fabric. If using words in the picture, remember to write the letters backward on the paper so they transfer correctly to the fabric.

Crayon Engraving

Crayons in many colors, including black
Paper
Sharp pencil

Have your child color an entire sheet of paper with crayons
in many colors, except black. When the paper is completely
colored, use a black crayon to color over the other colors.
Show your child how to use a sharp pencil to press down
firmly on the paper and engrave a picture or write a message.
The pencil will scrape off the black crayon, letting the colors
below show through.

If you like, use only white, blue, and gray crayons for the
first layer. Add the black layer, then scrape through it to
make a nighttime scene.

Foil Engraving

Scissors
Cardboard
Newsprint
Aluminum foil
Tape
Knitting needle or other engraving tool (dull pencil, handle
end of a spoon, key, and other rounded objects)
Colorful matte board or construction paper (optional)

Cut the cardboard to the size you want your engraving to be.
Cut several sheets of newsprint to the same size as the cardboard. Tear off a large sheet of aluminum foil, a little longer
than twice the length of the cardboard. Double the foil, place
the sheets of newsprint on top of the foil, then place the
cardboard on top of the newsprint. (The newsprint acts as a
cushion and helps prevent the engraving tool from cutting
through the foil.) Wrap the edges of the foil around the cardboard and tape them to the back. Turn the cardboard over
and smooth any wrinkles in the foil.

Show your child how to use a knitting needle or other
engraving tool to draw gently on the foil. Vary the tool he
uses, as different tools make entirely different lines. If you
like, mount the finished engraving on colorful matte board
or construction paper.

Thumbprint Flowers

This is a nice way to decorate a greeting card or make a spring scene.

Stamp pad
Paper
Crayons or markers

Press your child's thumb onto a stamp pad and then press it onto paper. Show him how to add petals, leaves, and a stem to make a flower from his thumbprint. Repeat this process on the same sheet of paper several times to make a garden scene.

If you like, use your own thumbprint to make a flower. Compare the size of your thumbprint with your child's.

Dribble Art

White glue
Construction paper, dark-colored and white
Chalk
Rubber cement
Glitter glue
Crayons or markers

Use one of the following methods to create a dribble art picture:

- Dribble white glue randomly or in a design on dark construction paper. When the glue is dry, have your child use chalk to color the spaces between the glue lines.
- Dribble rubber cement randomly or in a design on construction paper. When the rubber cement is dry, have your child use chalk to color over the whole sheet. Peel off the rubber cement to see the design.
- Dribble glitter glue randomly or in a design on white construction paper. When the glue is dry, have your child color the spaces between the glue lines with chalk, crayons, or markers.

Bleach Pictures

For this activity, be sure to wear old clothing and supervise carefully.

Spoon
Liquid bleach
Colored construction paper
Cotton swab or old toothbrush
Straw (optional)
Dark-colored marker or crayon (optional)

Drop a spoonful of bleach onto the paper. Before the bleach soaks into the paper, show your child how to spread it around with the spoon, a cotton swab, or an old toothbrush. If you like, have him gently blow through a straw to disperse the bleach in all directions. Watch as the color slowly fades wherever bleach has soaked into the paper.

If you like, when the bleach is dry outline the shapes or add accents with a dark-colored marker or crayon.

Coffee Filter Art

This activity is quick to set up and easy for even the youngest toddlers to do.

Washable markers
Coffee filter or paper towel
Eyedropper or sponge (optional)

Set your child in his highchair or at a low table and give him the washable markers and a coffee filter. The absorbency of the paper will make the colors blur as he draws on it.

If you like, have your child use an eyedropper or sponge to wet the coffee filter afterward to blur the colors even more.

See-Through Art

Crayons or markers   *Flat container*
Paper   *Sponge or paper towel*
Cooking oil

Have your child draw on the paper. Turn the paper over. Pour a small amount of cooking oil into a flat container. Dip the sponge into the oil and rub it on the back of the paper. Tape the transparent paper to a window to display.

Sugar Drawing

Sugar
Baking sheet
Flour, salt, chocolate drink mix, or Jell-O mix (optional)

Lightly sprinkle sugar on a baking sheet. Show your child how to use his finger to draw in the sugar. If you like, draw a letter, number, or shape in the sugar with your finger and have him copy it. Gently shake the baking sheet to make the drawing disappear, then start again.

If you like, use flour, salt, chocolate drink mix, or Jell-O mix instead of sugar.

Colored Photos

Markers, crayons, or colored pencils
Photocopies of family photos
Scissors, glue, and plain or construction paper (optional)

Let your child color photocopies of family photos. If he likes, cut out the photos and combine them to form a funny picture. Glue them onto paper, or use them to make unique greeting cards.

Balloon Art

Permanent markers
Balloon
Tape and table (optional)

Have your child use permanent markers to draw a picture or design on a balloon. If you like, stretch the balloon and tape it to a table to make a larger drawing surface. When the marker has dried, inflate the balloon to see the picture grow.

Soap Powder Pictures

Pencil
Construction paper
Newsprint or other paper
Soap powder
Glue

Have your child draw a simple design on the construction paper. Lay newsprint on your work surface. Pour a small amount of soap powder into a mound on the newsprint.

Beginning with a small section of the design, help your child trace the drawn lines with glue. Flip the paper over and gently press the glued section into the soap powder (or sprinkle soap powder over the paper). Remove the excess powder by tapping the paper gently. Repeat this process until the picture is complete. When the glue is dry, hang the picture to display it.

CHAPTER 3
Painting

Painting is just another way of keeping a diary.
        —Pablo Picasso

A child's love of painting begins at an early age and lasts for many years, if not a lifetime. A clean sheet of paper, jars of paint in vivid colors, paintbrushes to wield as she wills— what could make a child happier?

If you prepare properly, you can enjoy this art experience, too. Before you begin a painting project with a child of any age, consider the following:

- Don't undertake a painting project with your child when you're tired, rushed, or otherwise unable to devote yourself fully to what your child is doing.
- Protect the work space appropriately. I cover the kitchen table with an old sheet and throw the sheet in the wash when the project is over.
- If you don't have an art smock or old large T-shirt for your child to wear, dress her in old clothes that can become painting clothes. (Even washable paints may not wash out completely, and a child who's painting shouldn't worry about keeping clean!)

- If you have a wall you don't care much about, cover a large section of it with contact paper. The contact paper will likely damage the wall if you try to remove it, so be careful where you put it. You can tape the painting paper directly to the contact paper, and any paint that gets on the contact paper will wipe up easily.
- You can make a tabletop easel by removing the top and bottom flaps and one side panel of a cardboard box and taping the remaining three side panels together to form a triangle. Tape the bottom of the easel to the table and attach paper to one of the sides.
- Work outdoors when possible and let nature inspire your child.
- When possible, let your child listen to music as she paints.
- String a clothesline in the laundry room or kitchen and use it to hang paintings with clothespins to dry.

The best paint for young children to use is tempera paint, or poster paint, which you can buy at any art supply store as a premixed liquid or as a powder you mix with water. You can also make tempera paint by using the recipes in Appendix A. Because too many colors may distract children, provide only a few colors at a time. Start with red, blue, and yellow, and teach your child how to mix these colors to create others.

Tempera paint blocks are also available. They're practical because they don't have to be diluted and they can't be spilled, making cleanup easier. Just dab them with a wet paintbrush and start painting. Plus, tempera blocks are economical and last a long time. However, your child will probably not find them as fun to use as slick liquid paints.

Empty baby food jars work well as paint jars. Prevent the jar from tipping and soak up any drips by cutting a hole in a sponge and fitting the jar in the hole. You can also make a simple paint palette by gluing plastic milk jug lids onto heavy cardboard. Pour a small amount of paint into each lid. For a more permanent palette, nail several baby food jar lids to a block of wood. Here are a few more tips to keep in mind when working with tempera paint:

- Adding water and dish soap makes paint easier to clean up.
- Adding liquid laundry detergent will help prevent paint from cracking.
- Adding liquid starch will make paint thicker.
- Adding condensed milk will give paint a glossy finish.
- Adding powdered alum can preserve paint.
- Adding salt, crushed eggshells, or coffee crystals gives paint texture.
- Adding baby powder extends the life of paint and adds a nice scent.
- Plastic cafeteria trays are ideal for toddlers to paint on, with or without paper.

You can purchase paper from any art supply store, but consider these alternatives: Try fine sandpaper for a grainy effect. Newsprint is a wonderful paper for painting, and you can buy roll ends cheaply from your local newspaper publisher. Visit a local printing shop and ask an employee if you can leave an empty box for a week or two. He or she may agree to fill it with all kinds of terrific paper that would otherwise be discarded. For finger painting projects, use the shiny side of freezer paper, which you can buy at any grocery store. It's much cheaper than special finger paint paper and works just as well.

Older children will enjoy more refined materials and techniques. Provide acrylic paints as well as tempera paints. Provide high-quality brushes in a variety of sizes. Encourage your child to paint on paper, fabric, matte board, and ceramic tile as well as on three-dimensional objects like rocks, terra cotta pots, wood blocks, cardboard boxes, and Popsicle sticks.

When your child's paintings are dry, be sure to display them prominently. Think of creative uses for some of her artwork. For example, many painting projects make wonderful gift-wrap or greeting cards.

Painting Fun

The following painting activities are suitable for children of all ages.

Clothespin
String
Paint
Paper
Marbles

Plastic spoon
Small containers
Drinking straw
Balloons
Toothpicks

- Have your child clip a clothespin around several strands of string, then dip the strands in the paint and drag them across the paper.
- Pour different colors of paint into separate small containers. Let your child drop marbles into the paint, scoop them out with a plastic spoon, and roll them across the paper.
- Drip thinned paint onto the paper. Have your child gently blow through a drinking straw to disperse the paint in all directions.
- Blow up balloons of various sizes and tie the ends. Have your child hold the tied end of each balloon, dip the balloon in paint, and press it onto the paper.
- Have your child dip toothpicks in paint and use them as paintbrushes. Glue the toothpicks onto the painting for a three-dimensional effect.

Dabber Painting

Bingo dabbers
Paper
Tempera paint
Empty roll-on deodorant bottle or shoe polish bottle
Dishwand

Available at most dollar stores, bingo dabbers are a quick alternative to paint and brushes. The ink isn't washable and doesn't flow as well as paint, but your child will still have fun dabbing and painting with these giant paint pens. When the bingo dabbers are out of ink, pry off their tops and refill them with thinned tempera paint. Or try these suggestions to make your own dabbers:

- Pry the top off a roll-on deodorant bottle. Fill it with tempera paint (mixed fairly thickly) and snap the top back on the bottle. Your child will enjoy painting with this homemade bingo dabber.
- Pour paint in the handle of a dishwand, then have your child use the sponge to dab and smear paint on paper.

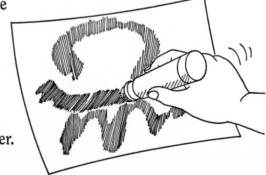

Squishy Paint

This activity isn't really painting, but it's a great alternative to the setup and cleanup required for a more traditional painting project.

Ziploc bag
3 tablespoons powdered
  tempera paint
¼ cup liquid starch
Finger paints

Ketchup, mustard, and/or
  mayonnaise
Corn syrup or whipped cream
Food coloring
Hair gel or shaving cream
Construction paper

Place one or more of the following combinations into a Ziploc bag:

- Powdered tempera paint and liquid starch
- Finger paints in different colors
- Ketchup, mustard, and/or mayonnaise
- Corn syrup or whipped cream and food coloring
- Hair gel or shaving cream and food coloring

Make sure the bag is well sealed, then show your child how to press the bag to make designs. Place construction paper under the bag (use a different color paper than whatever's in the bag) and notice how the color of the mixture seems to change.

Water Painting

Thick black marker
Coffee filter or paper towel
Water

Eyedropper
Paintbrush or sponge
(optional)

Have your child draw a picture or shape with the marker on a coffee filter or paper towel. Show her how to drop water from an eyedropper onto the drawing and watch the colors seep out.

If you like, have her apply water to the drawing with a paintbrush or sponge.

Shake Painting

Plain paper
Coffee can with lid
Paint

Small objects like rocks,
*   marbles, beads, pennies,*
*   and so on*

Put the paper around the inside of the coffee can. Pour a small amount of paint into the can. Drop in a couple of small objects. Replace the lid and have your child shake the can up and down and from side to side. Remove the lid and look to see the design. If you like, add more paint, replace the lid, and shake the can again.

If you like, make more paintings using a potato chip tube container, shoebox, or diaper wipe container.

Crumpled Paper Painting

Newspaper or tissue paper
Tempera paint
Plain paper

Glitter (optional)
Puffy Paint (optional)

Have your child crumple newspaper or tissue paper into a ball and dip it in the paint. Press the paper ball lightly on plain paper. If you like, sprinkle the paint with glitter before it dries, or use Puffy Paint (see Appendix A) instead of tempera paint.

Scented Paint

Packages of unsweetened Kool-Aid or Jell-O mix in a variety
* of colors*
Warm water
Small cups
Paintbrush, sponge, fingers, or other painting tool
Paper

Mix each package of mix with 2 teaspoons of warm water in a separate small cup. Stir until the mix is dissolved. Have your child use a paintbrush or other tool to paint the colors on paper.

Food Coloring Fun

Water
Shallow container
Food coloring
Coffee filter or paper towel
Paintbrush, old toothbrush, eyedropper, sponge, spoon
Construction paper

Pour water into the container and add enough food coloring to it to achieve the color you want. Have your child paint the mixture on a coffee filter or paper towel in the following ways:

- Use a paintbrush.
- Flick it from an old toothbrush.
- Apply it by drops from an eyedropper.
- Dab it on with a sponge.
- Pour it on with a spoon.

Let the painting dry, then mount it on construction paper and display it. Or use it to make a Beautiful Butterfly (see page 272).

Powdered Paint

For a painting activity, this one is pretty clean and requires little preparation.

Clothespin   *Spray bottle*
Cotton balls   *Water*
Powdered tempera paint   *Shallow containers*
Paper   *Hair spray*

Clip a clothespin onto a cotton ball, then have your child paint with it using the following methods:

- Dip the cotton ball into the powdered tempera paint and dot it onto the paper. Use several different colors of paint. When the painting is done, spray it with water and allow it to dry.
- Pour a small amount of powdered tempera paint into a shallow container. Pour a small amount of water into another container. Dip the cotton ball into the water, then into the paint, then press it onto the paper.
- Sprinkle a few colors of powdered tempera paint onto the paper. Use the cotton ball to spread the paint around the paper. When the painting is done, spray it with hair spray to set the paint. It will make a nice greeting card.

Puffy Painting

This paint gives artwork a three-dimensional effect.

Puffy Paint (See Appendix A.)
Squeeze bottles
Paper
Small spoon
Eyedropper
Paintbrush
Straw

Have your child use the Puffy Paint in one of the following ways:

- Pour the paint into squeeze bottles, then squeeze it onto the paper.
- Use a small spoon to drip the paint onto the paper.
- Drip paint onto the paper with an eyedropper.
- Apply the paint with a paintbrush.
- Thin a small amount of paint with water and drip it onto the paper with a spoon. Gently blow through a straw to disperse the paint around the paper.

Swat Painting

Here's a terrific idea for a hot summer day.

*Nontoxic, biodegradable paint (necessary because paint will
    soak into ground water)*
Baking pan or baking sheet
Fly swatter
Bucket of water and sponge or hose (optional)

Pour the paint into the baking pan or on the baking sheet.
Show your child how to dip the fly swatter into the paint
then slap the paint onto tree trunks, the fence, the sidewalk,
and so on. If you like, use a bucket of water and sponge or a
hose to clean the painted surfaces. Your child will enjoy
cleaning herself up in a kiddie pool or by running through
a sprinkler.

Ice Painting

"Paint with water" book   *Popsicle mold*
Baking pan   *Powdered tempera paint,*
Ice cubes   *Kool-Aid mix, or Jell-O mix*
Water   *Large sheet of paper*

- Place a "paint with water" page in a baking pan. Add ice cubes, and let your child move the pan around and watch the picture come to life.
- Freeze water in a Popsicle mold. Remove the ice Popsicles from the freezer a few minutes before using them, to let them to melt slightly. Have your child rub the ice Popsicles over the pages of a "paint with water" book.
- Make ice Popsicles as described above. Sprinkle a little powdered tempera paint, Kool-Aid mix, or Jell-O mix on the paper. Have your child paint a picture by rubbing the ice Popsicle in the paint.
- Mix 1 part powdered tempera paint with 1 part water and pour the mixture into a Popsicle mold. Remove the paint Popsicles from the freezer about 10 minutes before using them, to let them to melt slightly. Let your child use them to paint a picture on the paper.

Create-a-Color

Red, blue, and yellow paint
3 paint containers or jars
3 eyedroppers or small spoons
Styrofoam egg carton
Popsicle sticks or plastic spoons
Paintbrush and paper (optional)

Pour a small amount of each color of paint into a separate paint container. Place an eyedropper or spoon in each container. Show your child how to create colors by combining different colors of paint. Have her use the eyedropper or spoon to drop the paint into the egg carton sections, then mix the paint with Popsicle sticks.

If she likes, she can use her newly mixed colors to paint a picture on paper.

Finger Painting

Finger paints
Finger paint, wax, or butcher paper

Finger painting is a wonderfully messy adventure that every child should experience after age two—or younger, if you can stand it! The amount of work required to set up and clean up never seems to merit the five minutes (or less) most children will spend at this activity. Be prepared for a great big mess, and make sure your child wears an art smock.

Wet the paper first to allow the paint to slide better. Drop some paint on the paper and let your child go at it. You can buy commercial finger paint or make your own using the recipes in Appendix A.

For variety, chill or warm the finger paint. Add salt, sand, or coffee crystals for texture. Your child can spread thick finger paint with a Popsicle stick or spoon.

If you like, have your child finger paint on a tabletop or highchair tray, then press paper on the paint to make a print to save. Plastic cafeteria trays are great surfaces for finger painting, or try painting on a window or mirror. (Adding dish soap to the paint makes cleanup easier.)

Bathtub Paint

If you have ceramic tile around your bathtub, the food coloring may stain the grout, so use caution with this activity. If you like, use these paints in a kiddie pool instead.

1 cup liquid hand soap, clear or white
2 teaspoons cornstarch
Small bowl or measuring cup
Ice cube tray or Styrofoam egg carton
Food coloring
Paintbrush (optional)

Mix the soap and cornstarch in a small bowl or measuring cup. Pour the mixture into each section of an ice cube tray or egg carton. Add food coloring to each section, one drop at a time, until you get the colors you want. Have your child apply the paint in the bathtub with paintbrushes or use it as finger paint.

Squashed Painting

Spoon
Paint (tempera, finger paint, Puffy Paint, or Corn Syrup
Paint—see Appendix A for last two options.)
White paper
Plastic wrap
Shaving cream, food coloring, and Popsicle sticks (optional)

Help your child use a spoon to dribble paint onto the paper.
Use several different colors. Place a sheet of plastic wrap over
the paint (make sure the plastic wrap covers the whole sheet
of paper). Use your hands to press and smooth the plastic
wrap over the paint, then carefully peel the plastic wrap off
to reveal the squashed painting.

If you like, instead squirt a few blobs of shaving cream
onto the paper. Add a few drops of food coloring to each blob,
and have your child swirl each blob slightly with a Popsicle
stick. Cover the painting with plastic wrap and smooth it as
described above.

Roller Painting

Construction paper
Spoon or eyedropper
Liquid tempera paint
Rolling pin

Fold the paper in half like a greeting card, then open it. Have your child use the spoon to drop different colors of paint onto one of the inside halves of the card. Close the card and have your child roll a rolling pin across the paper to spread the paint inside. Open the card and let your child use her imagination to decide what the painting looks like. When the paint is dry, fold the card so the paint is on the outside.

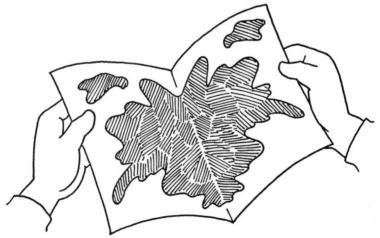

Dipping Designs

Colored ink, food coloring, or strong watercolors
Small containers
Paper doilies, paper towels, coffee filters, or other absorbent
  paper
Glue (optional)
Construction paper (optional)
Clear contact paper (optional)

Pour the ink, food coloring, or watercolors into small containers. Use two or three different colors (one color per container) for best results. If using ink or food coloring, thin it with a little water. Fold a paper doily or other absorbent paper into a small triangular or rectangular shape. Have your child dip each corner of the shape into a bowl of color for just a second or two. Dip each corner in a different color. Unfold the paper and hang it to dry.

  If you like, make a doily collage by gluing several dry doilies onto construction paper. Hang the collage to display, or cover it with clear contact paper to make a place mat.

Whipped Cream Finger Paint

*Whipped cream or vanilla
   pudding*
Paper

Food coloring
*Shaving cream and
   tempera paint (optional)*

Place whipped cream onto a tabletop, highchair tray, or sheet of paper. Add a few drops of food coloring for finger paint fun.

   If your child doesn't have sensitive skin and isn't likely to lick her fingers, use shaving cream and tempera paint instead, if you like.

Syrup Paint

Paintbrush
*Corn Syrup Paint
   (See Appendix A.)*

Heavy paper or poster board
Food coloring (optional)

Have your child paint with Corn Syrup Paint on the paper or poster board. When the paint is dry, it will shine beautifully.

   For an edible version of Corn Syrup Paint, omit the soap and use food coloring instead of paint. Use it as finger paint.

Spray Painting

Spray bottle
Water
Paint
Old sheet

Large sheet of newsprint or a
brown paper bag, cut to
lie open
Fabric paint
White T-shirt or other fabric
item

- Fill a spray bottle half with water and half with paint. For creative outdoor fun, hang an old sheet on a fence or clothesline and have your child spray-paint it.
- Have your child spray several different colors of paint onto newsprint or a paper bag. Let the painting dry and use it as gift-wrap.
- As an easy alternative to tie-dyeing, dilute fabric paint in a spray bottle and have your child spray it on a white T-shirt.

Crystal Painting

Paintbrush
Crystal Paint (See Appendix A.)
Dark construction paper

Have your child paint a winter scene with Crystal Paint on the paper. When the painting is dry, it will have an icy-looking, crystalline finish.

Nighttime Painting

Sponge or paintbrush
Heavy paper or cardboard
Black paint
Fluffy Soap Paint (See Appendix A.)
Popsicle stick or paintbrush

Use a sponge or paintbrush to completely cover the heavy paper with the black paint. Let the paint dry. Show your child how to use her fingers or a Popsicle stick to spread Fluffy Soap Paint on the paper to create a nighttime scene. Lay the painting flat to dry.

Shiny Paint

Condensed-Milk Paint (See Appendix A.)
Food coloring
Paintbrush
Paper
Pushpins
Bulletin board
Baking sheet
Small spoon

Divide a batch of Condensed-Milk Paint into portions and use food coloring to tint each portion a different color. Paint with it using one of the following methods:

- Have your child paint the paper with several colors. While the paint is still wet, pin the paper to a bulletin board or wall. The colors will run together for an interesting effect.
- Place the paper on a baking sheet. Have your child use a small spoon to drop several colors of paint onto the paper. Rotate the baking sheet so the colors flow together.

Michelangelo Painting

Tape
Large sheet of drawing paper
Low table
Paint
Paintbrushes

Tape the paper to the underside of a low table. Have your child lie on her back underneath the table and paint the paper.

Blob Painting

Sponge
Water
Paper
Paintbrush
Paint or food coloring

Dip the sponge in water and squeeze out the excess. Rub it across the paper until the paper is completely wet. Have your child dip a paintbrush in the paint, then hold it over the wet paper. As the paint drips onto the wet paper, it will spread into blobs.

Mirror Painting

Adding a little liquid dish soap to the finger paint makes cleanup easier!

Plastic tablecloth or old sheet
Full-length or unbreakable mirror
Finger paint
Wet paintbrush or cotton swab (optional)

To protect your carpet or flooring, place a plastic tablecloth under a full-length mirror. (Or purchase an unbreakable mirror from a camping supply store and place it on your child's highchair tray or on a table.) Let your child dip her hands in finger paint then paint on the mirror. When the paint dries, have her dab a wet paintbrush or cotton swab on the painted design and make new designs on the mirror.

If you like, on a warm day let your child finger paint on the outside of a glass patio door or low window. When the paint dries, have her use a wet paintbrush to make a design on the paint. Cleaning up with a sponge and bucket of water or garden hose can be part of the fun.

Negative Painting

Textured objects (lace doilies,   Tempera paint
*   paper dolls, leaves, or   Paintbrush*
*   cardboard cutouts of letters, Sponge*
*   numbers, or shapes)   Toothbrush*
Glue   Spray bottle
White paper

Gather a collection of textured objects. Dab glue on each object and stick it onto the paper. Have your child use one of the following methods to make a negative painting of the object:

- Use a paintbrush to paint the paper and the objects.
- Dab a sponge into paint, then press it onto the paper and the objects.
- Use a paintbrush or toothbrush to spatter paint over the paper and the objects.
- Use a spray bottle to spray-paint the paper and the objects.

When you've finished painting, remove the objects to see the negative images.

You can make a unique greeting card by first folding the paper in half, then using one of the above techniques to paint the front of the card.

Spatter Painting

This is a pretty messy way to paint, so be sure your work area is well protected, or paint outdoors if you can. Use this technique on any object you wish to decorate, such as paper, a terra cotta pot, a cardboard box, and so on.

Old toothbrush
Thin paint (tempera or acrylic)
Popsicle stick
Object to decorate

Dip the toothbrush's bristles in the paint, then hold the brush over the object to decorate. Have your child draw the Popsicle stick across the bristles, swiping it toward herself so the paint spatters the object, not her! Move the brush and swipe the Popsicle stick across the bristles again. Keep moving the brush until the spatters are spread across the object. Repeat this process with different colors.

Textured Painting

Paint
Paper
Large paintbrush

Cork
Dry sponge
Fork

Paint the paper, and when the paint is almost dry, use the following techniques to create a textured painting.

- Have your child roll a cork across the paper.
- Have her dab a dry sponge across the paper.
- Have her drag the prongs of a fork across the paper.

Striped Painting

Paint in at least 4 colors
Paintbrush

Paper
Markers (optional)

Show your child how to paint vertical stripes across the width of the paper, alternating between 2 or more colors. When the paint is dry, have her paint horizontal stripes down the length of the paper, alternating between 2 or more colors. Notice how the colors change where they overlap.

If you like, use markers instead of paint.

Comb Painting

Rubber or metal comb
Utility knife or sharp scissors (optional)
Sturdy cardboard (optional)
Tempera or acrylic paint
Paper, cardboard, or other object to decorate
Large paintbrush (optional)

If you don't have a comb, you can make one. Use a utility knife or pair of sharp scissors to cut a row of comb teeth along the side of the cardboard. Have your child dip the comb in the paint, then drag it across the surface of the object to decorate. Use different colors and drag the comb in different ways to make interesting designs and patterns.

If you like, use a large paintbrush to paint the entire surface of the object with thick paint. Drag a comb across the wet paint to make lines.

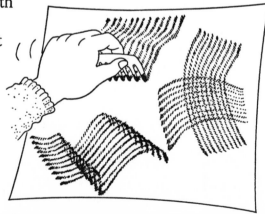

Magnet Painting

Shallow box
4 unopened food cans
Paper
Paint in several colors

Spoon
Small metal objects (paper
    clips, coins, keys)
Bar magnet

Place a can under each corner of the box. Lay the paper in the box and drip spoonfuls of paint onto the paper. Place the objects in the box and show your child how to use them to paint a picture by moving the magnet under the box.

Ball Painting

Newspaper
Large sheet of paper
Paint

Shallow containers
Assorted balls (tennis,
    golf, Koosh)

Spread newspaper on a sidewalk or other large surface. Lay the paper on the newspaper. Pour the paint into the container. Use a different container and ball for each color of paint. Have your child paint with the balls:

- Dip a tennis ball into paint, then bounce it on the paper.
- Dip a golf ball into paint, then roll it across the paper.
- Dip a Koosh ball into paint, then press it onto the paper.

Salt Painting

Paint   *Paper*
Paintbrush   *Salt*

Have your child paint a picture on the paper. While the paint is still wet, sprinkle salt all over the paper. Let the paint dry, then shake off the excess salt. You can either leave the picture as it is for a textured effect, or brush off the salt for a grainy effect.

Glue Design

White glue   *Tempera paint*
White construction paper   *Rubber cement (optional)*
Paintbrush

Have your child dribble the glue randomly or in a design onto the paper. Allow the glue to dry, then have her paint over the glue in one or more colors. The glue lines will stay white.

If you like, use rubber cement instead of glue. When the painting is dry, peel off the rubber cement to reveal white spaces.

Faux Gilding

Pencil
Thin cardboard or wood
  picture frame
White craft glue

Paintbrush
Gold acrylic paint
Soft cloth
Black shoe polish

Have your child draw a simple picture or pattern on the
cardboard or frame. Squeeze glue onto the drawn lines, then
let the glue dry for several hours or overnight (it leaves a
raised line when dry). Have your child paint the entire surface gold. When the paint is dry, use a soft cloth to rub black
shoe polish all over the painted area. Rub off the polish to
reveal an antique finish.

Milk Paint

Milk Paint (See Appendix A.)
Wood plaque or object, piece of wood, or paper
Paintbrush or sponge

Divide the paint into portions and use food coloring to tint
each portion a different color. Your child can paint the wood
or paper with a paintbrush or sponge, or use the paint in any
of the painting activities listed in this chapter.

Tipped Painting

Eyedropper or spoon
Liquid tempera paint
Large sheet of paper or a brown paper bag, cut to lie open
Squeeze bottle or straw (optional)

Have your child use an eyedropper or spoon to drip paint on the paper. Tip the paper in different directions to make a design. Drip on another color and tip the paper again for an interesting result.

If you like, have her disperse the paint by squeezing air from a squeeze bottle onto it or blowing through a straw.

Rainbow Painting

The wet paper really makes the colors flow and blend for a beautiful effect.

Paper *Paints and paintbrushes or*
Water *washable markers*
Wide paintbrush or sponge

Paint the paper with water using a wide paintbrush or a wet sponge. Your child can paint lines of color across the page with paints, or draw on it with washable markers.

Funny Feet

Newspaper
Large sheets of butcher or finger paint paper
¼ cup liquid tempera paint or finger paint
Old rubber boots or old tennis shoes
Old socks
Bucket of warm soapy water and towel
Shallow container (optional)

Cover your floor with newspaper, then spread the paper glossy side up on the newspaper. Pour the paint onto the paper. Encourage your child to paint in one or more of the following ways:

- Walk, stamp, and slide barefoot through the paint.
- Don old rubber boots or old tennis shoes, then walk and jump through the paint.
- Put on an old pair of socks, then walk, stamp, and hop through the paint.

Use more than one color of paint if you like. Have a bucket of warm soapy water and a towel ready for cleanup.

   If you like, pour paint into a shallow container. Have your child—barefoot or with shoes, boots, or socks—step first into the paint then onto the paper.

Broom Painting

Paint
Shallow container
Large sheet of drawing
  paper or newsprint

Broom
Damp string mop (optional)

Pour the paint into the container. Spread the paper on a sidewalk or other flat surface. Have your child dip the broom's bristles into the paint, then paint the paper with them.

If you like, use a damp string mop instead of a broom.

Spaghetti Painting

Small amount of spaghetti
Cooking oil
Paint

Shallow container
Paper

Cook and drain the spaghetti. Toss the noodles with a little oil to keep them from sticking together, and let them cool. Pour the paint into the container. Let your child dip some noodles into the paint then drag them across the paper. If you like, have her use several colors of paint.

CHAPTER 4
Printmaking

To live a creative life, we must lose our fear of being wrong.
—Joseph Chilton Pearce

Printmaking is fun and doesn't require a lot of artistic skill or coordination. By repeatedly making prints, children can develop an appreciation of texture and design. Generally, older toddlers and preschoolers will enjoy making prints, but very young toddlers probably won't understand the process. They tend to use the object to be printed like a paintbrush.

You can brush or roll paint onto the object to be printed, dip it in paint, or press it on a print pad. Make a print pad by wadding up newspaper and soaking it in liquid tempera paint, or place a thin sponge in a shallow container and cover it with paint. Use an ink pad for some printmaking projects. All kinds of paper can be used for printing, but newsprint, construction paper, and brown paper bags are some of the cheaper options. To cushion a print, place newspaper under the paper on which the impression is to be made. Encourage your child to press the object gently into the paint and then onto the paper to make a successful print.

Printing Fun

Liquid tempera paint
Shallow container
Paper or newsprint
Pint-size berry basket

Toy cars or trucks with
* wide wheels*
Empty thread spools
Duplo pieces in various sizes
Wine bottle cork

Pour a small amount of paint into the container, then try one of the following printmaking techniques. If you like, use paint in several different colors.

- Place the bottom of the berry basket into the paint. Have your child press it on the paper.
- Place a toy car or truck into the paint and roll it back and forth so the wheels are covered with paint. Have your child roll the toy across the paper.
- Dip thread spools in paint and have your child press them on the paper.
- Place a Duplo piece upside down in the paint, then have your child press it on the paper. Use both sides of the Duplo piece and use different pieces and different colors of paint for an interesting design.
- Dip one end of the cork in the paint. Have your child press it on paper.

Object Prints

Glue
Small objects (dry pasta, cereal, and so on) or textured
  materials (lace, rickrack, bubble wrap, and so on)
Small blocks of wood
Liquid tempera paint
Shallow container
Paper
Glitter and newsprint (optional)

Glue a small object or textured material onto one end of each wood block. Pour a small amount of paint into the container. Have your child press the objects into the paint then onto paper to make a design. Move the block around in different directions, and use different colors of paint to vary the design.

If you like, press the objects into glue, then onto paper. Sprinkle the paper with glitter and let the glue dry. Large sheets of newsprint covered with glitter make nice gift-wrap.

Scouring Pad Prints

Liquid tempera paint in
2–3 colors
Shallow containers
Plastic scouring pad

Paper
Scissors, plastic mesh,
small foam ball or sponge,
and twist-tie (optional)

Pour the paints into separate containers. Have your child dip the scouring pad into the paints and dab it onto the paper.

If you like, cut a piece of plastic mesh large enough to wrap around a small foam ball or sponge. Secure the ends with a twist-tie. Dip the ball or sponge into the paint and dab it onto the paper.

Chalk Prints

Cheese grater, blender, or
sandpaper
Chalk

Sponges in various sizes
Water
Construction paper

Grate chalk, process it in a blender, or rub it on sandpaper to create a fine powder. Soak the sponges in water and squeeze out the excess water. Have your child press them into the powder then onto the paper to create prints.

If you like, draw with chalk on a damp sponge, then press the sponge onto the paper to create a print.

Paint Roller Prints

Liquid tempera paint
Shallow container
Scissors
Craft foam
Glue
Empty paper towel or
  toilet paper roll

Paper or brown paper bag,
  cut to lie open
Sand, sugar, salt, or other
  fine-grained material
String
Foam paint roller

Use one or more of the following ideas to make a paint roller.
Pour the paint into a shallow container wide enough to fit
the roller.

- Cut stars, hearts, Christmas trees, or other shapes from
  craft foam. Glue the shapes onto the paper towel or toilet
  paper roll. Have your child dip the shapes in the paint
  then roll them on the paper or paper bag.
- Cover an empty paper towel or toilet paper roll with glue,
  then roll it in sand or other fine-grained material. When
  the glue is dry, have your child dip the roll in the paint,
  then roll it on the paper for a textured, dappled effect.
- Tie string around a foam paint roller. Have your child dip the
  roller in the paint, then roll it on the paper to make stripes.
- Cut out chunks from a foam paint roller. Have your child
  dip the roller in paint and roll it on the paper to make a
  thick solid pattern with holes.

String Prints

Liquid tempera paint
Shallow container
Paper
Pencil or marker
Small blocks of wood or
* 2- to 3-inch squares of*
* corrugated cardboard*
Glue
Small paintbrush (optional)

Scissors
String or rope

Pour the paint into the container. Make one or both of the following stamps, then have your child press them into the paint and onto paper to make a print.

- Draw a simple design or geometric shape on each block or square. Squeeze glue on the design or brush glue on it. Press string in the glue so it follows the design. Let the glue dry. Use a different design for each block and different colors of paint to create a one-of-a-kind string print.
- Wrap string or rope several times around a wood block. Make sure the string is distributed evenly, not gathered in one spot. Tie it in place. When printing, be sure to move the block around in different directions, and use different colors of paint to vary the design.

Tissue Paper Prints

Thinned paint *Scissors*
Paintbrush *Tissue paper*
Paper *Black marker (optional)*

Paint one side of the paper completely. Cut shapes from a contrasting color of tissue paper. Help your child press the shapes into the wet paint, leave them for a minute or so, then peel them off. The color from the tissue paper will be left in the paint. If you like, outline the shapes with black marker.

Eraser Block Prints

Utility knife
White erasers
Paint
Shallow container
Paper, note cards, or other surfaces on which to print

Use a utility knife to carve a design or pattern into one or more erasers. Pour a small amount of paint into the container. Have your child press the erasers into the paint, then onto the paper or other printing surface.

Paint Prints

Finger paint (See Appendix A to make your own.)
Plastic tabletop
Small objects, toothbrush or paintbrush, or drinking straw
  (optional)
Large sheet of paper

Place a small amount of finger paint on a plastic tabletop and
have your child paint with it. If you like, have your child
press objects into the paint, use a toothbrush or paintbrush
to make a design, or gently blow through a straw to disperse
the paint into a design. When your child's design is complete, have him wash and dry his hands thoroughly, then
place the paper on top of the finger painting. Have him rub
the paper all over. Slowly lift the paper off the table and hang
the painting to dry.

Printing Press

Most of the printmaking activities in this chapter involve pressing an object into paint then onto paper. But you can also make a one-of-a-kind print by pressing paper onto the design to be copied, much like a printing press does.

Tape and bubble wrap
Acrylic or tempera paint
Muffin pan
Printing ink
Baking sheet
Popsicle stick, pencil, or other drawing tool
Paintbrush
Paper

- Tape bubble wrap to the table or work surface. Have your child paint on the bubble wrap, then press paper on it to create a print of his design.
- Place a muffin pan upside down on a protected surface. Have your child paint the bottoms of the muffin cups. When he's done, lay paper on the muffin pan and press to make a print.
- Spread printing ink on a baking sheet. Have your child draw designs in the ink with a Popsicle stick or other drawing tool. Lay paper over the designs, press, and peel off the paper to reveal the print.

Soda Can Prints

Glue
String, rickrack, or lace
Soda can
Bubble wrap
Glue gun
Beads or small dry pasta
Liquid tempera paint
Shallow container

Paper
Coffee crystals, grated
  chocolate, ground
  cinnamon, flavored tea
  leaves, Jell-O mix, or
  other scented material
  (optional)

Use one or more of the following methods to make a soda can stamp.

• Wrap or glue string, rickrack, or lace around the can.
• Glue bubble wrap around the can.
• Use a glue gun to glue beads or small dry pasta onto the can.

Pour the paint into the container, then have your child roll the can in paint and then on paper. Use several colors of paint and roll the can in several directions for an interesting print. If you like, pour coffee crystals or other scented, textured material into another container. Roll the can in the paint, then in the material. Roll the can on the paper for a colorful, textured print with a delicious scent.

Sponge Prints

Scissors
Small thick sponges
Clothespins
Liquid tempera paint

Shallow container
Paper
Fabric paint and T-shirt or
cloth napkin (optional)

Cut the sponges into various shapes. In the center of each sponge, cut two slots for clothespins, making the slots about ¼ inch deep and ¾ inch apart. Clip the clothespins to the sponges for handles. Pour the paint into the container. Have your child dip the sponges into the paint and press them onto the paper. For a holiday project, use seasonal shapes and colors.

If you like, use fabric paint instead of tempera paint and press the shapes onto a T-shirt or cloth napkin.

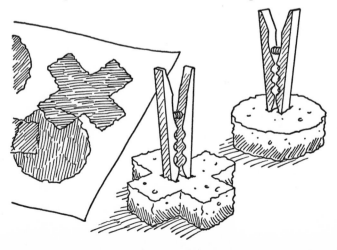

Bungee Prints

¼ cup sand or kitty litter
Knee-high pantyhose
Liquid tempera paint

Shallow container
Paper

Pour the sand or kitty litter into the pantyhose, then knot it near the opening. Pour the paint into the container. Have your child grab the knot, dip the sand-filled end into the paint, dangle it above the paper, then thrust it toward the paper. The sand-filled end will hit the paper, leave a print, and bounce back up.

Printed Place Mat

Scissors (optional)
9-by-12-inch sheet of craft foam
Fabric paint in shallow container

Cut the craft foam to a different size if you wish. Dip your child's hands or feet into fabric paint and have him press them onto the foam. Use fabric paint to add his name, his age, the date, or any message you like. When the paint is dry, use the foam as a place mat.

Crayon Prints

This activity requires a food warming tray or electric griddle. It's suitable for an older preschooler who's closely supervised by an adult.

Food warming tray or electric griddle
Aluminum foil
Oven mitt or thick glove
Crayons, paper removed
Paper
Damp cloth

Cover the warming tray or griddle with aluminum foil and set the appliance on low. Cover your child's non-dominant hand with an oven mitt or thick glove and have him hold the foil still with that hand. With his drawing hand, have him rub a crayon slowly on the warm foil to make a design. Remind him to keep his bare skin off the warming tray or griddle.

When his design is complete, show him how to carefully press paper onto the design and lift it off to make a print. Wipe the foil with a damp cloth and repeat the process to make a new print.

Corncob Prints

For this activity you may use either a fresh or dried corncob, with or without kernels.

Liquid tempera paint
Baking sheet
Corncob (husk removed)

Corncob holders (optional)
Paper

Pour the paint onto the baking sheet. Have your child grab each end of the corncob (or inserted corncob holders, if you like), then roll the corncob in the paint until it's completely covered. Have him roll the corncob back and forth or in different directions on the paper. If you like, pour another color of paint onto another baking sheet and repeat the process with the same corncob or a new one.

Alphabet Prints

This is a quick, easy way to make invitations, announcements, thank-you cards, and holiday greetings.

Cereal or dry pasta in
*   alphabet shapes*
Small mirror (optional)
Glue
Small block of wood
Liquid tempera or
*   acrylic paint*

Shallow container
Paper or note cards
Matte board or heavy
*   cardboard (optional)*
Paintbrush (optional)

Decide what message you want to write, then select the letters you'll need. Arrange the letters, then carefully reverse them so they are backward and the message reads right to left. (If you like, use a small mirror to check that the message's reflection reads correctly.) Glue the letters onto the wood block to make a stamp. Pour a small amount of paint into the container. Have your child gently press the stamp into the paint then onto the paper to make a print. Repeat this process as many times as you like.

If you like, arrange the letters on matte board or heavy cardboard. Glue the letters in place, remembering to reverse the letters and their order so they'll print correctly. Brush tempera paint on the letters, then press paper on them and rub gently to transfer the paint to the paper.

Sandpaper Prints

This activity requires an iron. Only an adult should handle the hot iron.

Sandpaper
Crayons
Newspaper
Ironing board
Iron
Plain paper

Have your child draw on sandpaper with crayons. Encourage him to press firmly and use vivid colors.

Place newspaper on the ironing board (or make a thick pad of newspaper and place it on a table or other work surface). Place the sandpaper on the newspaper and cover it with plain paper. Iron the paper until the crayon on the sandpaper has melted onto the paper.

To make another print of the same drawing, have your child color the design again and repeat the ironing process with another sheet of paper.

Fruit and Vegetable Prints

Paring knife
Various fruits and vegetables
Liquid tempera paint
Shallow container
Print or stamp pad (optional)
Plain or colored paper

Cut fruits and vegetables into halves, quarters, circles, or other shapes. Apples cut in half horizontally will have a star design in the middle (where the seeds are), while green peppers cut in half horizontally make great shamrock designs. Cut a potato in half and carve out a relief design: circle, square, heart, and so on. If you make letters, don't forget to carve them backward so they'll print correctly.

Pour a small amount of paint into the container. Have your child dip the shapes into the paint or press them on a print or stamp pad, and then press them onto the paper.

Textured Prints

For any of the printing projects in this chapter, you can substitute liquid tempera paint with Fluffy Soap Paint for a textured print.

Fluffy Soap Paint (See Appendix A.)
Textured objects (scouring pad, block, berry basket, cork,
   corncob, sponge, and so on)
Construction paper

Spread the paint onto the paper, then have your child press objects into the paint to make textured prints.

Button Prints

Glue   *Liquid tempera paint*
Assorted buttons   *Shallow container*
Small wooden dowels   *Paper*

Glue the buttons onto the dowels. Pour the paint into the container. Have your child dip the buttons into the paint then press them onto the paper. If you like, use several colors of paint and continue making button prints until the design is complete.

CHAPTER 5
Modeling, Sculpting, and Papier-Mâché

Creativity is...seeing something that doesn't exist already. You need to find out how you can bring it into being and that way be a playmate with God.

—Michele Shea

Modeling and sculpting activities create three-dimensional structures from a variety of materials. Such activities challenge a child's imagination, and playing with clay and other modeling compounds can also encourage his interest in science. (Science experiments often begin as hands-on activities.) The activities in this chapter use different modeling compounds and techniques to create interesting and beautiful pieces of art.

Papier-mâché is a special kind of paper modeling that uses a combination of paper and paste. Paper like newsprint, paper towels, gift-wrap, crepe paper, tissue paper, construction paper, or aluminum foil is torn into 2-inch or larger squares or long strips. (Torn edges glue better than cut edges and yield a more interesting finished appearance.) Paper and paste are layered on a mold, such as an inflated balloon, an empty toilet paper roll, or even crumpled newspaper. When the paste is dry, the papier-mâché art is removed from the mold.

Although papier-mâché activities can be messy and complicated, most modeling and sculpting activities—for example, sculpting with play dough or modeling clay—can be quite simple. For young children, the appeal is usually the sensory experience of working with the dough or clay, of squishing and shaping it with no other purpose than to feel the material in their hands. Let your child enjoy the material's texture and smell. Focusing on the outcome of any activity can make children feel they can't create well enough, and they lose their motivation to continue.

While most of the materials in this chapter are nontoxic, you'll need to supervise toddlers carefully and remind them not to eat the dough or clay. If nibbling is a problem, use edible materials like bread dough or Peanut Butter Play Dough (see page 197).

For any of the activities that call for clay, you can make your own using the recipes in Appendix A, or look for store-bought clay like Fimo or Sculpey that can be oven- or air-dried.

Molded Ornaments

Baker's Clay (See Appendix A.)
Drinking straw (optional)
Baking sheet
Fine sandpaper
Paint, markers, or glitter
Clear acrylic spray or clear
  nail polish
Fine wire or ribbon (optional)

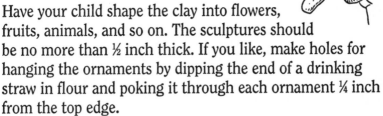

Have your child shape the clay into flowers,
fruits, animals, and so on. The sculptures should
be no more than ½ inch thick. If you like, make holes for
hanging the ornaments by dipping the end of a drinking
straw in flour and poking it through each ornament ¼ inch
from the top edge.

   Preheat your oven to 250°F. Place the ornaments on an
ungreased baking sheet and bake them for about 30 minutes.
Turn and bake them for another 90 minutes until they're
hard and dry. Remove them from the oven, let them cool,
then smooth them with fine sandpaper. Let your child decorate them with paint, markers, or glitter. Finish them with
clear acrylic spray or clear nail polish. If hanging the ornaments, loop fine wire or ribbon through the holes.

Cinnamon-Applesauce Ornaments

This dough shouldn't be eaten. Make sure your child doesn't make it a snack!

1 cup applesauce
1½ cups plus more ground
  cinnamon
⅓ cup white glue
Rolling pin

Cookie cutters
Flour
Drinking straw
Baking sheet or wire rack
Fine wire or ribbon

Mix the applesauce, 1½ cups cinnamon, and glue in a bowl. Refrigerate the dough for 1 hour. Sprinkle more cinnamon on a cutting surface and roll the dough until it's ¼ inch thick. Help your child cut out shapes with cookie cutters dipped in flour. Make holes for hanging the ornaments by dipping the end of a drinking straw in flour and poking a hole through each ornament ¼ inch from the top edge.

Preheat your oven to 150°F. Place the ornaments on a baking sheet and bake them for 6 hours. Or place them on a wire rack and let them air-dry for 2 days. To hang the ornaments, loop fine wire or ribbon through the holes.

If you like, make a garland by poking 2 holes about ½ inch apart at the top center of each ornament. When the ornaments are dry, weave ribbon through the holes and hang them to display.

Cookie Cutter Ornaments

Baker's Clay (See Appendix A.)
Rolling pin
Flour
Cookie cutters
Drinking straw
Baking sheet
Fine sandpaper
Paint, markers, or glitter
Clear acrylic spray or clear nail polish
Fine wire or ribbon

Roll the clay on a lightly floured cutting surface until it's ¼ inch thick. Help your child cut out shapes with cookie cutters dipped in flour. Make holes for hanging the ornaments by dipping the end of a drinking straw in flour and poking it through each ornament ¼ inch from the top edge.

Preheat your oven to 250°F. Place the ornaments on an ungreased baking sheet and bake them for about 30 minutes. Turn and bake them for another 90 minutes until they're hard and dry. Remove them from the oven, let them cool, then smooth them with fine sandpaper. Let your child decorate them with paint, markers, or glitter. Finish them with clear acrylic spray or clear nail polish. Loop fine wire or ribbon through each ornament and hang it to display.

Soap Fluff

Fluffy Soap Paint (See Appendix A.)
Heavy paper or cardboard
Popsicle stick or plastic knife
Cake decorator or cookie press
Ziploc bag

Have your child mold Fluffy Soap Paint on heavy paper or cardboard in one of the following ways:

- Mold it with her fingers.
- Spread it with a Popsicle stick or plastic knife.
- Squeeze it out of a cake decorator or cookie press.
- Spoon it into a Ziploc bag, seal the bag, then cut off a corner of the bag. Squeeze the bag to force the paint out.

Allow her creations to dry, then display them.

Squish Squash

2 cups water
Saucepan
½ cup cornstarch
Mixing spoon
Food coloring
Ziploc bags
Scissors and craft foam
Small seashells and beads (optional)

Boil the water in a saucepan. Add the cornstarch and stir it until smooth. Stir in a few drops of food coloring, adding more until you get the desired color. Remove the pan from the heat and cool the mixture. Use it in one of the following ways:

- Let your child squish it on her highchair tray or tabletop.
- Pour the mixture into 2 Ziploc bags and seal them. Your child can squish the bags or trace letters, numbers, or shapes on the outside of the bags.
- Create an ocean scene by coloring the mixture blue. Pour it into a Ziploc bag and add a few fish shapes cut from craft foam. If you like, add a few small seashells and beads. Seal the bag, then let your child squish it to make the fish swim.

Soap Clay

1 bar Ivory soap, grated
Water
Medium bowl
Food coloring (optional)

Soap mold (optional)
Tape, cookie cutter, and
  baking sheet (optional)

Combine the soap with a small amount of water in the bowl.
If you like, add a few drops of food coloring. Have your child
mix and squeeze the mixture with her hands, adding more
water if necessary, until it forms a ball. Have her shape the
clay with her hands, or press it into a soap mold or into a
cookie cutter taped to a baking sheet. Let the sculpture dry
and use it as soap.

Soap Mush

Toilet paper
1 bar Ivory soap, grated

Large bowl
Water

Tear a roll of toilet paper into thin strips. Pour the grated
soap into the bowl and add the toilet paper strips. Have your
child mush the strips with the soap and enough water to get
a moldable consistency. Let her mold the mush into whatever
shapes she wants, then let them dry.

Bread Clay Sculptures

6 tablespoons white glue
½ teaspoon liquid laundry
detergent
6 slices white bread, crusts
removed

Food coloring (optional)
Acrylic paints and paintbrush
Clear acrylic spray or
clear nail polish

Put the glue and detergent in a bowl, add the bread, and have your child knead the mixture until it's no longer sticky. If it's too wet, knead in more bread. If you like, separate the mixture into portions and tint each portion with food coloring. Let your child shape the clay into small figures. Let the sculptures air-dry for a day or two, then paint them. Finish them with clear acrylic spray or clear nail polish.

No-Bake Clay Sculptures

Modeling Clay or No-Bake
Craft Clay (See
Appendix A.)

Tempera or acrylic paint
Paintbrush
Clear acrylic spray

Have your child shape the cooled clay however she likes. Let the sculptures dry overnight. Decorate them with paint, and when the paint is dry, finish them with clear acrylic spray.

Magical Mystery Mud

This is a great compound for kids of all ages. It looks solid, but when you try to grab it, it just drips through your fingers.

1 box cornstarch
Bowl
Water
Food coloring
Shallow container
Toy cars
Measuring cups and spoons

Pour the cornstarch into a bowl. Add just enough water to stir the mixture, then add the food coloring. Use the mixture in one of the following ways:

- Have your child grab a handful of the mixture and let it drip through her fingers.
- Pour it in a shallow container and let her run her toy cars through it.
- Have her use measuring cups and spoons to measure and pour it.

Marshmallow Shapes

Glue or Ornamental Frosting (See Appendix A.)
Colored or white marshmallows, miniature and large sizes
Tempera or acrylic paints and paintbrush (optional)
Toothpicks (optional)

Help your child glue the marshmallows together to make simple or complicated shapes. Try forming letters, numbers, or basic geometric shapes. If you like, challenge your child to see who can build the most elaborate house, the most interesting car, or the funniest animal. Use colored marshmallows, or paint your shapes when they're complete.

If you like, use toothpicks instead of marshmallows, or use them with the glue to join the marshmallows together.

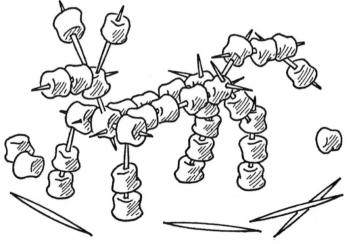

Cardboard Construction

Construction materials like cardboard boxes, cartons, paper
cups and plates, paper bags
Glue, tape, stapler
Texture materials like newspaper, tissue paper, construction
paper, gift-wrap, fabric and felt scraps
Decorating materials like paint, markers, stickers, crayons,
beads, feathers, sequins, yarn, ribbon, string, buttons

Have your child build a unique structure, using a variety of
materials. Let him experiment with ways to arrange the
materials (like stacking or nesting them) or ways to join
them (like gluing, taping, or stapling them). He can add texture with crumpled-up newspaper, tissue paper, gift-wrap,
and so on. He can decorate his structure with paint, markers,
stickers, beads, sequins, feathers, and so on.

Snow Sculptures

This activity is perfect for cold snowy days!

Dishpan or bucket
Snow
Heavy towel
Baking sheet or plastic tray
Food coloring (optional)

Fill a dishpan with snow and bring it inside. Lay a towel on the work surface to catch the drips, set a baking sheet on the towel, then pile some snow on the baking sheet. Your child will have fun sculpting the snow, shaping it into balls, packing it into measuring cups, molding it into mountains and running toy cars over it, and so on. If you like, mix in a little food coloring to make colored snow.

Styrofoam Structures

Toothpicks
Styrofoam shapes in
various sizes
Glue

Yarn and scraps of fabric,
paper, tissue paper, and
gift-wrap
Markers or paint
Scissors

Help your child use the toothpicks and Styrofoam shapes to make one or more of the following structures:

- Connect round, square, and rectangular shapes with toothpicks to form people. Glue yarn and fabric scraps onto the people to make hair and clothes. Use markers or paint to add facial features and other details.
- Connect three balls to make a snowman. Glue on fabric scraps to make a hat and scarf. Glue on paper scraps or use markers or paint to add facial features.
- Connect the shapes to form letters and numbers. Decorate them with paint or markers, or glue on tissue paper or gift-wrap scraps.
- Challenge your child to make a unique structure or object.

Sugar Cube Mosaic

Acrylic or tempera paint
Paintbrushes
Sugar cubes
Glue
Plywood or heavy cardboard

Help your child paint the sugar cubes in a variety of colors. If you like, paint the sides of each cube one color and then paint its top a contrasting color. (The bottom doesn't need to be painted because it'll later be glued onto the plywood base.)

When the cubes are dry, arrange them in an interesting pattern on the base. Leave a border on all four sides of the base. Apply glue directly onto the base, or brush it onto each sugar cube, then press the cubes into place. Paint the border a dark color.

Sugar Cube Shapes

Sugar cubes
Glue or Ornamental Frosting (See Appendix A.)
Heavy cardboard or Styrofoam meat trays
Pencil or marker (optional)
Paintbrush
Food coloring or liquid tempera or acrylic paint

Help your child use the sugar cubes in one or more of the following ways to create unique sculptures:

- Glue them randomly onto heavy cardboard.
- Build a house, tower, or castle with them. Decide on the layout you want, then glue the first row of cubes onto heavy cardboard. Add additional rows to make walls, leaving space for doors, windows, and so on.
- Glue them onto heavy cardboard to make letters, numbers, or shapes. If you like, draw outlines of the shapes on the cardboard first.

Paint your sculptures with food coloring or paint.

Sandcasting

Sand
4 cups plus more water
Small objects like shells,
   driftwood, leaves, and
   bottle caps
Bucket

6 cups plaster of Paris
Paint stick or wooden spoon
Short length of wire (optional)
Paintbrush and acrylic paints
   (optional)
Clear acrylic spray (optional)

Dig a hole about 12 inches square and about 6 inches deep in the sand. Wet the sides of the hole well. Press objects into the sides and bottom of the hole. Remove the objects, leaving their impressions, or leave them. (Objects left in the sand make depressions in the plaster. Impressions in the sand make raised areas in the plaster.) You can also build sand formations or make depressions in a sand pile in the hole.

Pour 4 cups of water into the bucket. Sprinkle the plaster of Paris over the water and stir the mixture until it's about as thick as pea soup. Pour plaster in the sand mold and wait for it to harden (about 30 minutes). If you'd like to hang the sculpture, stick a small wire loop into the plaster before it hardens.

Carefully remove the plaster from the sand mold. Brush away excess sand. If you like, have your child paint the plaster with acrylic paints. Then spray the plaster with clear acrylic spray.

Pasta Sculptures

If your child is likely to eat the glue-covered pasta, substitute the glue with corn syrup thinned with a little water.

White glue
Small containers
Liquid tempera paint or food coloring
Cooked pasta in a variety of shapes
Styrofoam meat tray
Cooking spray
Ribbon or yarn (optional)

Decide how many colors of glue you want to make, and pour glue into that number of containers. Add a few drops of paint or food coloring to each container, a different color per container. Have your child dip the pasta, one piece at a time, into the glue and lay it on the meat tray that's been sprayed with cooking spray. Repeat the process, using different colors of glue, until the sculpture is complete. When the pasta is dry, remove the sculpture from the tray.

If you like, hang the sculpture with ribbon or yarn to make a mobile.

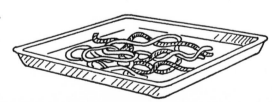

Positive Plaster Imprints

Play dough (See Appendix A to make your own.)
Shallow box or old baking pan
2 cups water
Bucket
3 cups plaster of Paris
Paint stick or wooden spoon
Paintbrush and acrylic paints (optional)
Clear acrylic spray (optional)

Press play dough into the bottom of the box or pan to make a smooth, flat surface. Press your child's hands or feet into the play dough to leave imprints. Pour the water into the bucket. Sprinkle the plaster of Paris over the water and stir the mixture until it's about as thick as pea soup. Pour a layer of plaster over the play dough and wait 10–20 minutes for the plaster to harden.

Now carefully remove the plaster to see raised relief of your child's hands or feet. If you like, have your child paint the plaster with acrylic paint. Then spray the plaster with clear acrylic spray.

Negative Plaster Imprints

Modeling clay (See Appendix
  A to make your own.)
Shallow box or old baking
  pan
Small objects like keys,
  coins, and leaves
2 cups water
Bucket

3 cups plaster of Paris
Paint stick or wooden spoon
Paintbrush and acrylic paints
  (optional)
Clear acrylic spray (optional)
Paper plate and picture hook
  (optional)

Press the clay into the box or pan to make a smooth, flat surface. Have your child press small objects into the clay.

Pour the water into the bucket. Sprinkle the plaster of
Paris over the water and stir the mixture until it's about as
thick as pea soup. Pour a thin layer of plaster over the
objects and let the plaster harden 10–20 minutes.

Now carefully remove the plaster. The objects will have
made an imprint in the hardened plaster. If desired, have
your child paint the plaster, then spray the plaster with clear
acrylic spray when the paint has dried.

If you like, pour the plaster onto a paper plate. Wait a
minute or two, then press your child's hand or foot gently
into the plaster. Hold for one to two minutes and remove.
Let the imprint sit overnight, then peel the plate from the
print. If desired, glue a picture hook onto the back and hang
the print on your child's wall.

Play Dough Balls

Play dough
Toy hammer
Toothpicks, Popsicle sticks, or thin plastic drinking straws
Large blunt needle (optional)
Clear nail polish or clear acrylic spray
String or elastic cord

Show your child how to roll play dough into balls, or for a very young child, roll the balls for him. Use the balls in one of the following ways:

- Roll them along a flat or gently sloping surface. Have a race to see whose ball reaches an agreed-upon point first.
- Line the balls up on your child's highchair tray or other surface. He'll have fun smashing the balls with a toy hammer.
- Stick toothpicks, Popsicle sticks, or thin plastic drinking straws into the balls to make porcupines or sea urchins.
- Roll the play dough into small balls to make beads. Pierce each bead with a toothpick or large blunt needle and allow them to dry for several days. Finish them with clear nail polish or clear acrylic spray, then thread them onto a length of string or elastic cord to create play dough jewelry.

Dough Play

Play dough (See Appendix A to make your own.)
Rolling pin and cookie cutters
Garlic press

Let your child play with the dough in one of the following ways:

- Flatten the dough with a rolling pin and cut it with cookie cutters.
- Roll the dough into ropes and use them to form letters or shapes.
- Sculpt figures out of the dough and use a garlic press to make play dough hair.

Putty Play

2 parts white glue   *Rolling pin (optional)*
1 part liquid starch   *Airtight container*
Small bowl

Combine the glue and starch in the bowl and mix them well. Let the putty dry until it's workable. (You may have to add a bit more glue or starch.) Let your child mold the putty into shapes or roll it with a rolling pin. Store it in an airtight container when she's done molding with it.

Clay Magnets

Food coloring (optional)
Salt Clay (See Appendix A.)
Rolling pin
Flour
Small plastic knife or
cookie cutters

Baking sheet
Tempera or acrylic paint
and paintbrush (optional)
Clear acrylic spray
Glue gun
Magnetic strips

If you like, add food coloring to a batch of Salt Clay. Use the clay in one or more of the following ways:

- Let your child use his imagination to shape the clay into small figures like animals, fruit, and so on.
- Have him roll the clay into ropes, then shape the ropes into letters or numbers.
- Roll the clay with a rolling pin on a floured surface, then use a small plastic knife or cookie cutters to cut out shapes.

Preheat your oven to 200°F. Place the figures on a baking sheet and bake them 1–2 hours, or until they're very hard. If you like, your child can paint the figures. Finish the figures with clear acrylic spray.

Use a glue gun to attach a magnetic strip to the back of each figure.

Clay Beads

No-Bake Craft Clay (See Appendix A.)
Toothpick or large blunt needle
Food coloring (optional)
Baking sheet
Table knife
String

Make a batch of No-Bake Craft Clay, and don't add food coloring to it.

Have your child roll the clay into small bead-size balls. Use toothpicks to poke holes through the middle of the beads. If you like, dip a toothpick in food coloring and decorate the beads before they dry. Place the beads on a baking sheet and allow them to dry for several hours or overnight.

If you like, marbleize the clay by forming it into a small loaf shape. Open up the loaf as you would a hot dog bun and pour several colors of food coloring into the opening. Close the loaf and press it a little to distribute the food coloring. Roll the clay into a log shape, cut it into slices, and follow the instructions specified above to make beads about ½ inch in diameter.

When the beads are dry, string them to make necklaces or other jewelry or use them for other craft projects.

Clay Tablets

*Clay that can be oven- or air-dried (See Appendix A to make
  your own.)*
Stick or pencil
Small objects that won't melt in an oven
Paintbrush and tempera or acrylic paint (optional)
Clear acrylic spray

Form the clay into a tablet shape roughly the size of a sheet
of paper. Have your child come up with a story, and use a
stick or pencil to write the story in the clay. Or press small
objects into the clay to make interesting designs.

   If using store-bought clay like Fimo or Sculpey, follow
the manufacturer's directions to dry the clay. If using homemade clay, follow the recipe directions for drying. If you like,
have your child decorate the tablet with paint. Finish it with
clear acrylic spray.

Clay Pot

Clay (See Appendix A to make your own.)
Spoon (optional)
Paintbrush and tempera or acrylic paint (optional)
Clear acrylic spray

Help your child use one of these methods to make a pot:

- Roll the clay into a ball and make a hole in the center with your thumb. Push outward from the hole with your thumb and press your fingers on the outside of the ball as you shape the pot, turning the clay as you work. Try to keep the clay the same thickness all the way around.
- Make long ropes of clay, each about as thick as a large crayon. Coil the ropes around and around, stacking the coils to make a pot shape. You can leave the pot as it is or use a spoon to smooth out the coils.

If you're using store-bought clay like Fimo or Sculpey, follow the manufacturer's directions to dry your pot. If using home-made clay, follow the recipe directions for drying. If you like, have your child decorate the dried pot with paint. Finish the pot with clear acrylic spray.

Papier-Mâché Beads

Papier-Mâché Paste (See Appendix A.)
Shallow container
Scissors
Newsprint or other paper
Knitting needle
Tempera or acrylic paints and paintbrush
Varnish or clear acrylic spray

Pour the papier-mâché paste into the container. Cut newsprint or other paper into long narrow triangles. Each triangle will make a bead. Dip each triangle in the paste and wrap it around a knitting needle, starting with the short edge. Continue wrapping it on top of itself to make a bead. Slip off the bead and leave it to dry. When the beads are dry, have your child decorate them with paint, and finish them with varnish or clear acrylic spray.

Papier-Mâché Bowl

Papier-Mâché Paste
  (See Appendix A.)
Shallow container
Cooking spray
Bowl
Scissors

Newsprint or other paper
Tempera or acrylic paint and
  paintbrush, colored tissue
  paper or gift-wrap, or glue and
  photos or magazine pictures
Varnish or clear acrylic spray

Pour the paste into the container. Spray cooking spray on the inside of the bowl. Cut at least eight pieces of newsprint (more for a thicker, stronger bowl) big enough to cover the bowl. Dip one piece into the paste, then press it onto the inside of the bowl. Smooth out any air bubbles or wrinkles. Help your child repeat this process until all the pieces are layered and the inside of the bowl is covered.

Allow the papier-mâché to dry for several days. Gently separate the papier-mâché from the mold and trim the edges with scissors. (The outside of the bowl will be smooth and the inside rough.) Paste two layers of small paper strips over the cut edge and allow them to dry.

Paint the bowl, paste on layers of colored tissue paper or gift-wrap, or glue on photos or pictures cut from magazines. Finish with varnish or clear acrylic spray.

If you like, turn the bowl you're using as a mold upside down and make a papier-mâché bowl on the outside surface. This will make a bowl with a smooth inner finish and rough outer finish.

Papier-Mâché Napkin Rings

Papier-Mâché Paste (See Appendix A.)
Shallow container
Scissors
Empty paper towel or gift-wrap roll
Newsprint or other paper torn into strips
Colored tissue paper or paint and paintbrush
Baby bottle or baby food jar (optional)
Cooking spray (optional)
Construction paper (optional)

Pour the papier-mâché paste into the container. Cut an empty paper towel or gift-wrap roll into 1-inch sections. Dip the paper strips into the paste, or brush paste onto the strips with a paintbrush. Help your child cover the cardboard ring with as many layers of paper and paste as you like. When the paste is dry, add colored strips of tissue paper and paste or paint the rings.

If you like, use a baby bottle or baby food jar instead of cardboard rings. Spray cooking spray on the outside of the bottle or jar, then mold newsprint strips and paste around it. Add a layer of construction paper strips and paste for strength, then add an additional 6 layers of paper strips and paste. Remove the bottle and finish the napkin ring by adding strips of tissue paper and paste or painting it.

Papier-Mâché Fish Piñata

Papier-Mâché Paste (See
Appendix A.)
Shallow container
Newsprint or other paper
Large balloon
String
Paintbrush (optional)
Small toys and candy

Scissors
Cardboard
Tape or glue
Colored tissue paper,
fringed crepe paper,
or paint and paintbrush
Dark-colored marker

Pour the paste into the container. Tear newsprint into long strips. Inflate the balloon and hang it from a string. Dip the strips into the paste or brush paste onto paper with a paintbrush. Press the strip onto the surface of the balloon. Help your child cover the balloon with many layers of strips and paste, leaving a hole about 6 inches in diameter on one side. Allow the piñata to dry for several days.

When it's dry, pop the balloon and pour in the toys and candy. Cut fish fins and a tail from the cardboard, and tape or glue them onto the balloon. Cover the opening, fins, and tail with more strips and paste. Let the piñata dry again, then decorate it with tissue paper, crepe paper, or paints. Add facial features with a dark-colored marker.

Papier-Mâché Pulp

Papier-mâché pulp is a claylike modeling material. Your child can use it to create papier-mâché objects without using a mold or to add dimension to other papier-mâché creations.

Scrap paper that's not shiny
(newsprint, newspaper,
copier paper, old letters)
Medium bowl
Boiling water

2 heaping tablespoons flour
½ cup plus more water
Small saucepan
Blender
Colander

Tear the scrap paper into small pieces. (Use colored tissue paper to make colored pulp.) Put the pieces in the bowl and cover them with boiling water. Soak them for 1 hour.

Combine the flour and water in the saucepan and stir until well blended. Cook, stirring constantly, until the mixture has boiled and become thick. Remove the pan from the heat and allow the paste to cool.

Put a small handful of the soaked scraps into the blender. Pour in additional water and blend on high for 15 seconds. Pour the pulp into a colander and repeat the process with another handful of scraps.

When all the scraps have been blended, press the pulp in the colander firmly to remove as much water as possible. Add 1 cup of pulp to the cooled flour paste and mix well.

Papier-Mâché Finger Puppets

Toilet paper roll
Narrow-necked bottle
Papier-Mâché Pulp (See page 127.)
Glue gun and yarn or Spanish moss (optional)
Acrylic paint and paintbrush

Place an empty toilet paper roll over the neck of the bottle. Help your child mold a head on the roll with Papier-Mâché Pulp. Include exaggerated facial features like a chin, nose, mouth, ears, and eyebrows. If you like, form hair from the pulp (or use a glue gun to attach yarn or Spanish moss when the puppet is dry). Let the puppet dry for several days. When it's completely dry, let your child paint it.

Papier-Mâché Creation

Paper containers like cardboard boxes, oatmeal containers,
  ice cream containers, egg cartons, and frozen juice cans
Wide masking tape or duct tape
Papier-Mâché Paste (See Appendix A.)
Shallow pan
Newspaper
Damp towel (optional)
Tempera paint and paintbrush or glue, fabric, and tissue
  paper

Help your child build an animal, make-believe creature, or
other object with the paper containers. Use wide masking
tape or duct tape to hold your creation together.

Pour the papier-mâché paste into a shallow pan. Tear the
newspaper sheets into strips (or in half, if your creation is
large). Briefly soak the strips in the paste, then press them
onto your creation. Smooth out the wrinkles with a damp
towel or your hands.

Continue adding strips until your creation is completely
covered. Let it dry for a day or so, then paint it or glue on
fabric and/or tissue paper details.

Papier-Mâché Pulp Objects

Papier-Mâché Pulp (See page 127.)
Petroleum jelly or cooking spray
Shallow bowl or plate
Frozen juice can or glass jar
Small cardboard box with lid
Acrylic paint and paintbrush (optional)
Clear acrylic spray

Help your child use the Papier-Mâché Pulp to create one or more of the following objects:

- For a bowl or plate that's smooth on the outside and rough on the inside, spread petroleum jelly or spray cooking spray on the inside of the mold and press the pulp onto the inside. For a product that's smooth on the inside and rough on the outside, turn your mold upside down, grease the outside of the mold, and press pulp onto the outside. Pat the pulp well to make an even, compact layer. Bring the pulp right to the rim of the mold and create an even edge.
- Use a frozen juice can or glass jar as a mold to make a vase. Grease the outside of the container or jar, cover it with pulp, patting it well to make a compact layer with an even top edge.

- Remove the lid from the cardboard box, grease the outside of the lid and box, and cover them with an even layer of pulp to make a keepsake box.

Let the pulp dry for up to a week before removing it from the mold. If you like, have your child paint the objects, and finish them with clear acrylic spray.

Papier-Mâché Piggy Bank

Papier-Mâché Paste
  (See Appendix A.)
Shallow container
Several sheets of
  newspaper
Balloon
Scissors

Empty paper egg carton
Glue
Pipe cleaner
Paintbrush
Pink paint
Black paint or marker
Utility knife

Pour the Papier-Mâché Paste into the container. Tear the newspaper into squares or strips, then inflate and tie the balloon. Have your child dip the squares or strips into the paste, then place them on the balloon, making sure their edges overlap. Cover the balloon with many layers of pasty paper and let it dry for a day or two.

Cut six sections from the egg carton. Glue one section onto the tied end of the balloon for the pig's nose. Glue four sections onto the underside of the pig for its feet. Cut the remaining section in half and glue one piece onto each side of the pig's head for its ears. Use a curled pipe cleaner for the pig's tail. Cover the nose, feet, ears, and tail with paper squares or strips and paste and let them dry.

Have your child paint the pig pink, and add details with black paint or marker. Use a utility knife to cut a money slot in the top of the pig.

Newspaper Fruit

Newspaper
Tape
Glue
Water
Shallow container
Tempera or acrylic paints and paintbrush

Help your child scrunch newspaper into fruit shapes. Use tape to hold the shapes together. Tear more newspaper into strips. Combine equal amounts of glue and water in the container. Dip the strips into the mixture and wrap them around the shapes. Cover the shapes completely with wet strips. Allow the shapes to dry, then let your child paint them. When the paint is dry, arrange the fruit in a basket or Papier-Mâché Bowl (see page 124).

If you like, shape people, animals, cars, and so on.

Newspaper Platter

This form of papier-mâché uses water rather than paste.

Plastic or glass platter or plate
8 single sheets of newspaper
Large container of warm water
Scissors
Liquid tempera, acrylic, or spray paint
Shellac or clear acrylic spray

Turn the platter upside down on a flat surface. Place a sheet of newspaper in the container of warm water. When the newspaper is soaked, remove it from the water and lay it over the platter. Shape it firmly to the platter and press it firmly along the edge.

Repeat the procedure described above with the remaining sheets of newspaper, being sure to alternate the direction of the paper for each layer. Let the newspaper dry.

When the newspaper is dry, it will lift off the platter easily and retain its shape. Lift off the newspaper platter and trim its edges with scissors. Let your child paint it, then finish with shellac or clear acrylic spray.

CHAPTER 6
Glue, Paper, and Scissors

Never tell people how to do things. Tell them what to do and they will surprise you with their ingenuity.
—George S. Patton, Jr.

Kids, glue, paper, and scissors are a great combination. Toddlers learn early in life that scrunching and tearing paper is a wonderful sensory experience. Preschoolers who have mastered the use of scissors enjoy the process of cutting and gluing, no matter what it is they're making. Older children can make an amazing variety of crafts from a simple supply of glue, paper, and scissors.

Keep the following suggestions and guidelines in mind when working on the activities in this chapter with your child:

- Keep a stack of old magazines on hand for tearing. (Most toddlers and young preschoolers can't yet handle a pair of scissors, so avoid frustration and tear everything.)
- Be on the lookout for old wallpaper books (decorating centers usually sell these fairly inexpensively). They're great for all the interesting shapes and patterns they contain. Cut out circles, squares, rectangles, triangles, or other creative shapes, and glue them onto construction paper to make designs and pictures.

- Buy your child a good pair of child's scissors and teach him how to use them safely.
- Vary the type of glue your child uses: a glue stick, bottled glue, or paste that can be spread. Pour a small amount of white glue into a baby food jar lid and mix in a drop or two of food coloring. Use a small paintbrush or cotton swab to spread the glue around.
- Provide your child with lots of interesting things to cut and glue on: greeting cards, fabric scraps, and paper scraps (tissue paper, gift-wrap, and construction paper). You can also use dry pasta, yarn, cotton balls, and ribbon. Outdoor walks can yield a wonderful supply of natural materials, including leaves, pine needles, flower petals, and so on.
- Vary the surface onto which your child sticks things: paper plates, cardboard, egg cartons, tissue boxes, and paper of all shapes, sizes, and colors.

The most important thing about working with glue, paper, and scissors is that your child should try to do the whole project by himself. Remember that the process is much more important than the product. Although the materials may be simple, working with glue, paper, and scissors will help develop small motor skills in young children and will challenge them artistically, too.

Salt Art

Salt
Powdered tempera paint
Empty saltshakers or spice containers
Glue
Paper
Small paintbrush or spoon
Colorful Creative Salt (optional)

Mix the salt with the paint in the shakers or containers, one for each color. Have your child brush glue on the paper with a paintbrush or dribble it on with a spoon. (Little ones may enjoy smearing the glue with their fingers.) Sprinkle the salt mixture over the paper. When the glue is dry, tip off the excess salt and hang the picture to display.

If you like, use Colorful Creative Salt (see Appendix A) instead of salt and paint.

Scrap Art

Child's scissors
Colorful paper scraps (gift-wrap, tissue paper, construction
  paper, and so on)
Glue stick
Construction paper
Clear contact paper
Glitter glue or thick black marker

Help your child cut or tear paper scraps into interesting
shapes, then use one or more of the following ideas to create
colorful artwork.

* Rub a glue stick onto construction paper, then press a
  paper shape onto the glued area.
* Press a paper shape onto clear contact paper that's been
  taped to the table sticky side up.
* Use glitter glue or a thick black marker to outline the
  edges of each individual shape.
* Use seasonal shapes and colors for a holiday collage (for
  example, cut hearts from red, white, and pink paper for
  Valentine's Day).

Spice Pictures

*Empty saltshakers or spice
  containers*
*Spices or other fine-
  grained material*

Small paintbrush or spoon
Glue
Paper

Fill the shakers with the spices. Have your child brush glue
on the paper or dribble it on with a spoon. (He may enjoy
spreading the glue with his fingers.) Shake the spices over
the paper. When the glue is dry, tip off the excess spices and
hang the picture to display.

Rice Art

Cotton swab or paintbrush
Glue
Heavy paper

Rice
*Food coloring, newspaper,
  and baking sheet (optional)*

Dip the swab or paintbrush in the glue and brush it across
the paper. Have your child sprinkle the rice on the glue, then
gently shake the paper to remove the excess rice.

If you like, color the rice before using it. Soak it in food
coloring, spread it on a newspaper-lined baking sheet, and
allow it to dry.

Froot Loop Art

*Food processor or rolling
   pin
Froot Loops cereal
Glue stick
Construction paper*

*Empty saltshaker or spice
   container (optional)
Clear contact paper
Hard candies or other
   crushable materials*

Process the cereal or crush it with a rolling pin. Have your
child use the crushed cereal in the following ways:

- Rub glue onto the paper, then sprinkle the cereal onto it.
  If you like, use a saltshaker to shake the cereal onto the
  glue. Tip off any excess.
- Pour the cereal onto contact paper that's taped to the table
  sticky side up.
- Crush other materials and use it as above.

Scissors Fun

*Stickers
Calculator paper
Child's scissors*

*Rubber stamps and
   stamp pad*

Have your child place stickers at various intervals on a strip
of calculator paper or stamp images along the strip. Let him
cut the paper between each sticker or image.

Funny Friend

Old magazines
Child's scissors
Glue
Paper
Popsicle sticks (optional)

Look through old magazines
and find pictures of people,
clothing, accessories, animals,
cars, and so on. Let your child
cut out the pictures however
he wants and glue them onto
the paper, perhaps attaching
the face from one person to the
body of another. Glue on clothing
and accessories. If you like, give
the funny friend a pet, house, car, or family members.

   If you like, cut out the funny friends and glue them
onto Popsicle sticks to make puppets.

Cutting Practice

Play dough *Paper*
Child's scissors *Pen or pencil*

- Roll play dough into rope shapes and have your child practice cutting the ropes into small pieces.
- Have your child practice cutting paper into strips then cutting the strips into smaller shapes.
- Draw an easy-to-cut pattern (using two parallel lines to form a path) on paper. Paths can make zigzags, S shapes, straight lines, and so on. Have your child cut along the center of the path without straying.

Shape Collage

Scissors *Glue*
Brightly colored paper *Black construction paper*
White paper

Cut a variety of shapes from the colored paper. Include geometric shapes, like circles, triangles, and squares, as well as other shapes like whorls, squiggles, and blobs. Have your child arrange the shapes on the white paper and glue them into place. Mount the collage on the black paper, or use paper in one of the bright colors you've included in the collage.

Food Collage

Old magazines and grocery store fliers
Scissors
Glue
Paper plate
Tape and pipe cleaner (optional)
Construction paper
Clear contact paper

Search through the magazines and fliers for pictures of your child's favorite foods. Cut out the pictures, then help your child do one or more of the following with the cutouts:

- Glue them onto a paper plate. If you like, tape a curved pipe cleaner onto the back and hang it to display.
- Make a place mat by gluing the pictures onto construction paper and covering it with clear contact paper.
- For toddlers, use clear contact paper instead of construction paper and glue. Tape the contact paper sticky side up to his highchair tray. Let him stick the cutouts onto the contact paper. When the collage is complete, cover it with another sheet of contact paper.

Family Collage

Family photos
Glue
Cardboard or colored construction paper
Child's scissors
Clear contact paper
Popsicle sticks (optional)

Sort through family photos for ones that can be copied
and/or ones your child may use. Young children will enjoy
simply gluing the photos onto cardboard or construction
paper. Older children may like cutting and trimming the
photos before gluing them onto paper. Cover the collage with
clear contact paper or have it laminated at a local print shop.

If you like, cut out the paper-mounted photos and glue
them onto Popsicle sticks to make puppets.

Circle Animal

Small circular objects (jar lids, plastic margarine container
 lids, cups, plates, and so on)
Colored construction paper
Pencil
Scissors
Glue
Black marker or crayon

Place the objects on the paper, trace around them, then cut
out the circles. Cut some of the circles in half. Challenge
your child to construct a real or imaginary animal by gluing
an arrangement of circles and half-circles onto paper.

If you like, cut out other shapes like squares, rectangles,
and triangles and challenge your child to build another
creature.

Sticky Collage

Here's a sticking project especially for toddlers.

Small can or plastic container
Scissors
Assorted kinds of tape (masking, cellophane, colored,
  and so on)
Construction paper
Colored labels and dot stickers

Turn the can or container upside down and use it as a tape holder. Cut or tear off various lengths of tape of different types and colors, and place them around the edges of the tape holder so your child can pull them off easily. Show your child how to pull off a piece of tape and stick it onto the paper. Let him add colored labels and dot stickers to the collage.

Sticky Dot Collage

Colored dot stickers
Colored paper
Small index cards

Use one of the following methods to create a sticky dot collage:

- Choose one color of dots and a contrasting color of paper. Have your child stick as many dots as desired onto the paper. When the collage is done, hang it and stand back to admire the design.
- Have your child stick a variety of dots onto dark-colored paper to create a mosaic effect. When the mosaic is complete, mount it on a slightly larger sheet of paper in a contrasting color and hang it to display.
- For seasonal greeting cards, fold colored paper in half. On the front of the card, have your child stick on dots in a design (for example, stick red dots in a heart shape for Valentine's Day, green dots in a shamrock shape for Saint Patrick's Day, and so on).
- To reinforce number and letter skills for preschoolers, draw the outlines of numerals and letters on small index cards. Have your preschooler fill in the outlines with dots.

Fabric Collage

Scissors
Fabric scraps
Pinking shears (optional)
Heavy paper
Glue
Marker (optional)

Cut the fabric scraps into small pieces. If you like, use pinking shears to create zigzag edges. Help your child arrange the scraps on heavy paper in a design or randomly. Glue them into place.

You can make this a seasonal activity by using fabric scraps in seasonal colors or patterns. Outline a shape (like a heart, shamrock, or Christmas tree) with a marker on heavy paper, then fill in the outline by gluing on the scraps.

Lantern Garland

This decoration starts with smaller pieces of paper but is made in the same way as a traditional paper lantern.

Several sheets of colored paper
Child's scissors
Pencil or pen (optional)
Glue or stapler
Ribbon

Fold the paper into quarters and cut the paper along the folds to make four rectangles. Fold each rectangle in half so the long edges meet, and show your child how to cut from the folded edge to within a half-inch of the opposite side. (You may want to draw a line to show where to stop cutting.) Have him make cuts along the fold, then unfold the rectangle and form it into a cylinder by gluing or stapling the short edges together. Make several lanterns in different colors, then thread them onto ribbon to make a garland.

Mosaic Art

This project is best done by older children or those who like to pay attention to detail. If your child has never made a mosaic, make a small sample to show him before he begins.

Scissors
Construction paper in many colors
Glue stick
Clear contact paper or shellac
Square or round colored labels (optional)

Help your child cut light- and bright-colored construction paper into ½-inch-wide strips, then cut the strips into ½-inch squares. Sort the squares by color, and have your child glue them onto dark-colored paper in any design he likes. He may want to start with a large central image, like a tree, flower, whale, or car, then fill in the background with a contrasting color. Explain to your child that the squares should not touch each other but should have only a tiny bit of space between them.

When the mosaic is finished, cover it with clear contact paper, apply a coat of shellac, or have it laminated. If you like, mount the mosaic on one or two larger sheets of colored construction paper to give it a border.

If you like, instead of using paper and glue, create a mosaic with square or round colored labels.

Homemade Stationery

Use scraps of wallpaper and gift-wrap to make your own stationery.

Child's scissors
Wallpaper or gift-wrap scraps
Glue
Note cards or plain paper
Envelopes
Construction paper

Have your child cut shapes from wallpaper or gift-wrap scraps. Glue the shapes onto note cards or plain paper and envelopes to create unique stationery. Or use the cutouts to decorate homemade greeting cards made from construction paper.

Envelopes

Envelopes made from gift-wrap or wallpaper add a special
touch to holiday cards, invitations, and thank-you notes.

Envelope
Gift-wrap or wallpaper
Pen or pencil
Scissors
Glue, tape, or stickers

Let your child choose an envelope the same size as the envelope he'd like to make. Help him carefully pull apart and
open the envelope flaps to create a flat pattern for tracing.
Lay the pattern on the wrong side of a piece of gift-wrap or
wallpaper and have your child trace it.

Carefully cut out the traced shape. Fold in the side flaps
and glue the bottom flap onto the side flaps. (Look at the
original envelope if you're not sure where to fold.)

Let your child place a card or letter inside the envelope
and seal it with glue, tape, or stickers.

Paper Border

Generations of children have enjoyed making paper-doll chains. Your child can use this technique to make a border for his bedroom, the mantel, or a plain wall in your home.

Scissors　　　　　　　　*Pencil*
Large sheet of paper　　*Crayons, markers, or paint*

Cut a strip of paper about 36 inches long and 6 inches wide. Fold the strip of paper accordion style, making each panel about 3 inches wide. Have your child draw a simple figure on the top panel. Make sure part of the figure touches the fold on each side. Carefully cut out the figure, making sure not to cut along the folds. Let your child unfold the chain of figures and decorate it with crayons, markers, or paint.

If you like, create seasonal borders by cutting out shapes like hearts, Easter eggs, stars, Christmas trees, and so on.

draw figure

but don't cut along folds!

cut along lines of figure through every panel

Rainbow Paper Chain

*Construction paper in rainbow colors (red, orange, yellow,
 green, light blue, indigo, and violet)*
Scissors
Glue or stapler

Cut each color of paper into strips 3–4 inches long and ½–1
inch wide. Have your child form a circle with one red strip
then glue or staple the ends together. Then have him take an
orange strip, loop it through the red strip, and glue or staple
the ends together. Repeat this process, using strips in this
order of color: yellow, green, light blue, indigo, and violet.
Begin the pattern again with a red strip, and repeat the
process until the chain is as long as your child wants. Use it
to decorate a doorway, wall, or mantel.

Gift Bag

Paper lunch bag
Stickers, used greeting cards,
* or gift-wrap*

Glue stick
Hole punch
Ribbon

Have your child decorate both sides of the bag with stickers or glue on designs cut from the cards or gift-wrap. Fold down the top of the bag twice, then punch two holes through all the folds. Open the bag to place the gift inside, then refold it. Thread ribbon through the holes and tie it in a bow.

Photo Puzzle

Photo, at least 5-by-7 inches
Heavy paper, cut to same
* size as photo*

Glue
Clear contact paper
Child's scissors

Glue the photo onto the heavy paper. When the glue is dry, cover the photo with clear contact paper. Let your child cut the picture into pieces to create his own puzzle.

If you like, have your child write a message on the back of the paper before he cuts it. Use it as a unique greeting card.

Paper Chain

As a kid, I remember saving colorful Wrigley's gum wrappers to make a classic gum wrapper chain. It's really a kind of origami and requires a lot of precise folding, which is tough for young children. The following is a larger, simpler version of the gum wrapper chain. Although it's a difficult process to describe, it's easy to demonstrate. Be sure to try it yourself before showing your child what to do.

2 sheets of different-colored construction paper
(8½-by-11 inches)
Scissors
Table

Fold each sheet of paper in half so the long sides meet. Unfold each sheet. Cut both sheets into strips ½–¾ inch wide and 8½ inches long. Take a strip and fold both ends inward so they meet at the middle, then close the middle fold. Repeat this process until all your strips are folded.

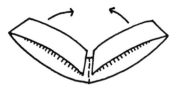

Lay a folded strip (A) on the table so its middle fold points away from you. Now grab a different-colored strip (B) and hold it so its middle fold points to the left. Thread the ends of strip B through the ends of strip A. Push strip B all the way to the right, then slide strip B away from you until it catches on the middle fold of strip A.

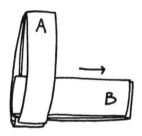

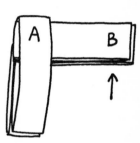

Grab another folded strip (C) and hold it so its middle fold points toward you. Thread the ends of strip C through the ends of strip B and push it all the way up.

Continue weaving strips together to make a long zigzag chain.

Decoupage Basket

Tissue paper, patterned or in complementary colors
Paintbrush
Decoupage glue
Small straw basket

Tear the tissue paper into small pieces. Use a paintbrush to
paint a thin layer of decoupage glue on the inside of the basket. Have your child quickly cover the glue with overlapping
tissue pieces. (If your child works slowly, use only a little
glue at a time.) Brush glue around the rim and on the outside of the basket and press tissue paper over the edges and
down the sides. Let the basket dry for about an hour, then
turn it over and repeat the process for the bottom of the
basket.

Paper Beads

Scissors
Colored paper, tissue paper,
  or gift-wrap

Plastic drinking straws
Glue
String or elastic cord

Cut the paper into strips as long as a drinking straw and about 2 inches wide. Have your child spread glue all over the wrong side of the paper. Lay the straw on the glue along a long edge of a strip. Roll the paper around the straw. Let the glue dry, then cut the straw into ½-inch sections. Repeat this process as many times as you want. String the beads to make necklaces and other jewelry.

Zigzag Strips

Scissors
Plain or colored paper or
  gift-wrap

Hole punch
String or elastic cord

Cut paper strips 6 inches long and 1 inch wide. Show your child how to fold each strip back and forth 5 times to make a folded packet about 1 inch square. Punch a hole through the center of the packet. (If the paper is too thick, punch through each fold separately.) Make several packets, then thread string through the strips to make a necklace.

Charm Bracelet

Paper clips
Scissors
Heavy paper or index cards
Hole punch
Magazine pictures or photos
Glue
Clear contact paper (optional)

Have your child join paper clips to make a bracelet that fits his wrist. Cut small shapes (like a circle, square, diamond, heart, star, and so on) from the paper or index cards. Punch a hole at the top of each shape. Cut magazine pictures or photos to fit on the shapes, and have your child glue them onto both sides of the shapes. If you like, cover each shape with clear contact paper, trim it, and repunch the hole. Slip a paper clip through each hole, then hook it to the paper clip bracelet.

If you like, combine charms with Paper Beads and Zigzag Strips (see page 159) to create a colorful necklace.

Art Book

Children can learn a lot about art just by looking at it, noticing details, and enjoying it. This activity allows your child to create his own book of art.

Magazines, newspapers, gallery catalogs, old calendars, and so on
Scissors

Glue or tape
Large scrapbook or paper
Stapler or three-hole punch and binder

Help your child find pictures of works of art in magazines, newspapers, and so on. Cut the pictures out and glue them into the scrapbook or tape them to the paper.

When you have a good collection of pictures, staple the pages together to make a book, or three-hole punch the pages and place them in a binder. Your child will enjoy looking at his art book and sharing it with others.

String Art

Liquid tempera paint
Liquid starch or white glue
Small container
Scissors
String
Construction paper
Drawing paper and crayons, papers removed (optional)

Mix the paint with an equal amount of starch or glue in the container. Cut the string into various lengths.

Show your child how to dip each string length into the mixture then arrange it on construction paper to make an interesting design.

If you like, after the string pictures are dry, place drawing paper over each design. Rub the side of a crayon on the paper to make a rubbing of the string design. Use several colors of crayons and move the paper to create an overlapping pattern.

CHAPTER 7
Nature Arts and Crafts

Think of all the beauty still left around you and be happy.
—Anne Frank

Young children need to be outdoors every day to use up some of their seemingly endless energy and to develop their large motor skills. Being in nature in all kinds of weather also inspires our creativity. Spend time outdoors together and learn to appreciate and enjoy the beautiful world in which we live.

When you're outdoors or planning nature arts and crafts projects for your child, here are some suggestions:

- Look for natural objects that can be used in arts and crafts projects: rocks in interesting shapes, bird feathers, pine cones, flowers, colorful leaves, and so on.
- Whenever possible, work outside and let nature inspire your child. Set up an easel on the porch and paint in nature's colors. Or mold play dough into the shape of a bird's nest.
- Take advantage of the seasons. Make a bird feeder when cold weather arrives. Paint the snow with food coloring. Collect fresh flowers in the spring and summer to dry and use later in the year.

3-D Nature Collage

Take your child for a walk in the woods or a park to collect interesting items with which to make a collage.

White glue
Natural objects (pebbles, bark, leaves, pine needles, pine
  cones, nuts, seeds, wood shavings, shells, and dried flowers)
Piece of wood, paper plate, or cardboard
Flat container and Popsicle stick or cotton swab
Food coloring (optional)
Glue gun (optional)
Clear contact paper (optional)

Glue natural objects onto a wood, paper plate, or cardboard base. Squeeze glue into a flat container and dab it onto each object with a Popsicle stick or cotton swab, or apply it directly from the bottle. Add food coloring to the glue, if you like. Older children may enjoy using a glue gun (with your supervision). When the collage is complete, let it dry overnight.

If you like, a very young child may enjoy sticking the objects onto clear contact paper that's been taped sticky side up to a table or highchair tray.

Flower Crown

Daisies or dandelions
Utility knife

Pick a bunch of daisies or dandelions with stems at least 3 inches long. Use a utility knife or your fingernail to make a small slit through each stem about 2 inches below the blossom.

Show your child how to slip the stem of one flower through the slit in the stem of another flower. Pull the flower through the slit. Slip the stem of a third flower through the slit in the second flower, and so on. Continue adding flowers to the chain in this way until it's the desired length. Twist the last stem around the first to form the chain into a crown or beautiful necklace.

Thirsty Celery

This is a good activity to show your child how plants drink water through their stalks and where the water goes.

Clear glass or vase
Water
Food coloring
Knife
Celery stalk
White carnation or daisy (optional)

Fill the glass or vase halfway with water and let your child add enough food coloring to tint the water a bright color. Trim the end of a celery stalk and place it in the water. Your child will enjoy watching the celery change color over the next few days.

If you like, use a white carnation or daisy in place of the celery.

Nature Collection

Objects found on nature walks make great supplies for arts and crafts projects. Collecting natural objects is also a fun way to learn about the natural world. Collections teach children to be observant and encourage skills like sorting and classifying. Help your child begin and organize a collection of natural objects.

- **Rocks:** Rock collectors hunt for specimens, carry out experiments, and learn how rocks, minerals, and fossils are formed. Whether your child wants to become a true rock collector or just use the interesting specimens she finds in her art projects, a book like *Rocks & Fossils* by Ray Oliver (Random House, 1993) will provide her with the information she needs to get started.
- **Leaves:** Collect a variety of fresh leaves. Preserve them by pressing, waxing, or rubbing them. (See page 173.) Identify your leaves with a book like Jim Arnosky's *Crinkleroot's Guide to Knowing the Trees* (Simon & Schuster, 1992).
- **Sand:** Each time you visit a beach, bring home sand in a large container to use for arts and crafts projects. Also, fill a small container like a pill bottle or film canister with the sand. Label the small container with the name of the beach and the date. At home, look at the sand with a magnifying glass. Compare it with other samples in your collection, noticing differences in color, texture, and grain sizes.

Nature Collage

Scissors
Clear contact paper
Clipboard or heavy cardboard
Tape
Masking tape (optional)

Cut clear contact paper to the same size as the clipboard. Tape the contact paper sticky side up to the clipboard. Head outdoors and explore, letting your child choose leaves, flowers, and other discoveries to attach to the sticky clipboard. At home, cover the collage with another sheet of clear contact paper and display it.

If you like, make a nature bracelet by wrapping masking tape sticky side up around your child's wrist. Have her attach her nature finds to the bracelet, then cut it off when you get home.

Nature Painting

Glue
Tempera paint
Feathers, pine cones, pine needles, flowers, and other
   natural objects
Paper

Mix a small amount of glue with the paint. Have your child use feathers and other natural objects to brush the paint onto the paper. Notice the different patterns made by each object. If you like, leave a few natural objects in the paint to make a three-dimensional collage.

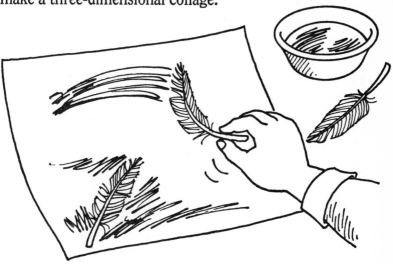

Rock Painting

Rocks
Paintbrush
Tempera or acrylic paint

Clear acrylic spray or clear
   nail polish
Small leaves

- Collect rocks in a variety of shapes and sizes. Have your child paint the rocks. If you like, finish with clear acrylic spray or clear nail polish when the paint is dry.
- Have your child paint one side of a small leaf. Press the painted side onto a smooth rock. Repeat this process several times, using different leaves and colors if you like. When the paint is dry, finish the rock with clear acrylic spray or clear nail polish and use it as a paperweight.

Mud Puddle Painting

Paintbrush
Paper

Old plastic tablecloth
Mud puddle

After a rainfall, head outside with paintbrush and paper. Find a mud puddle and spread an old plastic tablecloth on the ground next to it. Lay the paper on the tablecloth, then have your child paint mud on the paper.

Snow Art

Snow
Loaf pan
Molds (buckets, ice cube
    trays, plastic containers,
    milk cartons, and so on)
Bucket of warm water

Food coloring or liquid
    tempera paint
Spray bottle full of water
Paintbrush and small
    containers (optional)

- Pack the snow into a loaf pan. (If the snow is powdery, sprinkle a little water on it before packing it into the pan.) Turn the pan upside down and tap the bottom lightly to release the snow loaf. Make several loaves and have your child use them to build a fort. Loaves laid with their long sides together will make a sturdy structure. Pack snow in the gaps between the loaves as you lay them.
- Fill the molds with water and set them outdoors overnight to freeze. Dip each mold in warm water for a few seconds to loosen the ice. Turn the mold upside down to slide the ice out. Let your child build an ice sculpture. (Be sure she wears mittens or gloves.) To stick two shapes together, spray water on the surfaces you want to join and hold them together for about 10 seconds.
- Add a few drops of food coloring or a spoonful or two of tempera paint to a spray bottle full of water. Let your child paint the snow by spraying it. Or she can brush on undiluted liquid tempera paint poured into small containers.

Mud Play

Most children will play with mud quite willingly. Here are a few creative mud activities to try.

Dirt　　　　　　　　　　　*Sturdy paper or plastic plate*
Water　　　　　　　　　　 *Table knife or spatula*
Bucket or other container　*Cake pan or pie pan*
Muffin pan　　　　　　　 *Grass or flower petals*

Mix clean dirt (without stones, grass, or any other materials) with water in a bucket. Use the mud in one or more of the following ways:

- **Mud Bricks:** Make the mud thick enough to form a mud ball. Press the mud into sections of a muffin pan. Preheat your oven to 250°F and bake the mud for about 15 minutes. Have your child stick the cooled mud bricks together with wet mud and build structures.
- **Mud Handprints:** Make the mud fairly thick. Fill a paper or plastic plate with mud and use a knife or spatula to smooth it into a flat, even surface. Have your child press her hand into the mud then remove it carefully. Place the handprint in the sun to dry.
- **Mud Pie:** Make the mud really thick. Give your child a cake pan or pie pan and let her make a mud pie. Decorate the pie with grass or flower petals and dry it in the sun.

Leaf Art

*Glue and liquid tempera
  paint or food coloring
Thinned colored glue
Paintbrush
2 equal-size sheets of
  wax paper*

*Colorful leaves
Flowers, pine needles, and
  other natural objects
  (optional)
Glitter
Hole punch and string*

Mix glue with paint or food coloring, or use colored glue
thinned with a little water. Paint the glue onto one sheet of
wax paper. The paper should be well coated with glue. Have
your child stick colorful leaves onto the paper. If you like,
add other natural objects. Sprinkle glitter over the leaves.
Paint glue onto the other sheet of wax paper, then place it on
top of the first sheet. Press the sheets together, punch a hole
near the top, then hang the picture with string in a window.

Leaf Stenciling

Leaves
Masking tape
Construction paper or
  poster board
Scissors
Sponge
Clothespin

Liquid tempera paint in fall
  colors (orange, yellow, red,
  and brown)
Shallow containers
Newspaper
Clear contact paper (optional)

Collect leaves in a variety of shapes and sizes. Stick rolled pieces of masking tape to the backs of the leaves and arrange them on construction paper or poster board. Press down gently on the leaves so they lie flat against the paper.

Cut the sponge into small pieces and clip a clothespin onto a piece. Pour the paints into separate containers. Show your child how to dip the sponge piece into the paint, blot it on newspaper to absorb the excess paint, then lightly dab it around the edge of each leaf. Use a new sponge piece for each color. When the paint is dry, carefully remove the leaves. Let the paint dry, then hang the picture to display. If you like, cover with clear contact paper to make a leaf place mat.

If you like, tape the leaves to a window or mirror, then dab paint around them. The paint can be removed easily with glass cleaner.

Flower Press

Pressed flowers can be used to decorate a variety of paper items.

Small flowers (pansies, violets, buttercups, daisies, and so on)
Newspaper or other absorbent paper
Heavy book
Glue
Plain note cards, note paper, or construction paper
Clear contact paper

Have your child pick an assortment of small flowers. Make sure she picks them when they're free of rain or dew. Place them between sheets of newspaper, making sure the flowers don't touch each other. Cover the paper with a heavy book. Leave the flowers for a week or so until they're completely dried.

To make stationery, have your child glue the pressed flowers onto plain note cards or note paper. She can also glue the flowers onto construction paper gift tags. To make a collage, have your child glue the flowers onto construction paper. Turn the collage into a place mat by covering it with clear contact paper.

Nature Bookmark

Follow the directions for Flower Press (page 175) to press fresh flowers, or use dried flowers instead.

Scissors
Window envelope
Construction paper
Pressed or dried flowers
Glue
Markers or gel pens
Hole punch and ribbon (optional)

Cut out the window with a narrow paper border from a window envelope. Cut construction paper to the same size as the window envelope cutout. Arrange the flowers on the construction paper cutout, then place the window on top of the flowers. Be sure the flowers show through the window. Remove the window and glue the flowers onto the construction paper. Squeeze glue on the paper border around the window, then press it into place on the construction paper. Have your child decorate the bookmark with markers or gel pens. If you like, punch a hole at the top of the bookmark, loop ribbon through the hole, and tie it.

Dried Flowers

Drying flowers is a wonderful way for your child to enjoy their beauty all year long.

Variety of flowers   *Florist's foam (optional)*
Rubber bands or string   *Vase or pot*
Clothes hangers

Choose a variety of flowers to dry. Some flowers that dry well are baby's breath, thistles, roses, strawflowers, statice, dahlias, black-eyed Susans, and poppies. Show your child how to use rubber bands or string to tie flower stems together in groups of five. Tie the bunches by their stems to clothes hangers. Be sure the bunches don't touch each other. Hang the coat hangers in a closet or in a dark, dry, well-ventilated room. The darkness prevents the flowers from fading, and the dryness and ventilation prevent the growth of mildew.

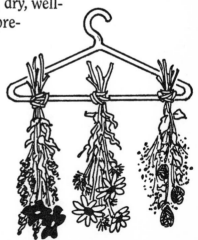

After about two weeks, the flowers should be dry. If you like, place a piece of florist's foam in a vase or pot to help hold the flowers in place. Arrange the flowers however you wish.

Leaf Print Note Cards

Paintbrush   *Blank note cards*
Paints   *Clean scrap paper*
Fresh small leaves

Have your child brush an even coat of paint on the back of a leaf. (For fun, use two or more colors of paint.) Place the leaf painted side down on the front of the note card. Place scrap paper on the leaf and rub it. Remove the paper and peel off the leaf to reveal the print. Repeat the process for each note card, using a different leaf or color of paint if you like.

Berry Ink

1 cup blueberries or   *1 teaspoon salt*
  blackberries, mashed   *Small saucepan*
½ cup water   *Sieve*
1 teaspoon vinegar   *Clean glass jar*

Combine the berries, water, vinegar, and salt in a small saucepan. Bring the mixture to a boil. Reduce the heat and simmer the mixture for 5–10 minutes. Let it cool, then pour it through a sieve and into the jar.

Let your child use it to paint on rocks or to do some of the painting or printmaking activities in Chapters 3 and 4.

Bird Buffet

Heavy string, yarn, or a
shoelace
Pine cone
Small plastic knife or
Popsicle stick
Peanut butter

Birdseed
Stale bread
Cookie cutter
Pencil or straw
Round oat cereal or pretzels

Use one or more of the following ideas to make a simple bird feeder:

• Tie heavy string, yarn, or a shoelace around the top of a pine cone, then knot it, leaving enough string to hang the pine cone. Have your child use a small plastic knife or Popsicle stick to thoroughly cover the pine cone with peanut butter, then roll it in birdseed.

• Have your child cut a shape from slightly stale bread with a cookie cutter. Spread peanut butter on the bread shape, then sprinkle on birdseed. Poke a hole close to the edge of the shape with a pencil or straw. Let the bread dry until it's hard, then loop string or yarn through the hole and tie it.

• Have your child string round oat cereal or pretzels onto heavy string, yarn, or a shoelace. When she's done, tie the ends together.

Hang the feeder outside near a window where your child can watch the birds eat.

Nest Depot

When birds build their nests, they use materials found in their environment. Set up a nest supply depot in your back yard to help them out.

Wire clothes hanger with cardboard tube
Contact paper
Scissors, construction paper, and tape (optional)
Utility knife
String, thread, and hair

Cover the cardboard tube with contact paper to protect it from the rain. (If you don't have a hanger with a cardboard tube, cover a 2-inch-wide strip of construction paper with contact paper, wrap it loosely around the bottom of the hanger, and tape it to form a tube.)

Cut a row of slits through both sides of the cardboard tube. Have your child stuff strands of string and thread through each hole so the ends hang out. Human hair is a great nest-building material, so clean your hairbrushes and stick the hair through the cardboard tube, too.

Place the hanger on a tree branch and watch for birds to take the supplies.

Twig Frame

Scissors
Cardboard
Construction paper or gift-wrap
Photo
Dry twigs
White glue
Ribbon

Cut cardboard and construction paper or gift-wrap rectangles about 2 inches longer and 2 inches wider than the photo. Glue the paper onto the cardboard. Break the twigs so you have two a little longer than the length of the cardboard and two a little longer than the width. Have your child glue the twigs onto the edges of the cardboard so they cross at the corners. Glue the photo onto the center of the frame. When the glue is dry, tie a ribbon end to each end of the top horizontal twig and hang the frame to display.

Painted Pebbles

Glue
Rocks
Paint
Paintbrush

Play dough or fabric scraps,
  ribbon, or lace
4 egg cartons

- Have your child glue rocks of various sizes together to make rock people or animals. Have her paint the rock creations and add accessories made from play dough, fabric scraps, ribbon, or lace.
- Collect at least 48 small rocks. Have your child divide the rocks into 4 equal sets and paint each set a different color. Paint each egg carton to match one set of rocks. Use the stones and egg cartons as a sorting game.

Shell Painting

Seashells
Paintbrush

Tempera or acrylic paint
Clear acrylic spray

Collect seashells in a variety of shapes and sizes (white ones work best). Let the shells dry in the sun, then have your child paint each shell. If you like, finish the shells with clear acrylic spray when the paint is dry.

Natural Dye

Large beet
Saucepan
1 quart water
Sieve
Bowl
4 tablespoons salt
White cotton socks or other cotton items
½ large red cabbage (optional)

Have your child wash the beet, then place it in the saucepan with the water. Bring the water to a boil and simmer for about 30 minutes. Pour the beet water through a sieve and into a bowl. Stir the salt into the beet water. Pour the beet water back into the saucepan. Place the socks in the beet water and simmer for about 20 minutes. Remove the saucepan from the heat and allow the socks to cool. Rinse the socks in cold water and hang them to dry. Wash the socks before wearing them.

If you like, use half of a large red cabbage instead of the beet.

Ice Ornament

Natural objects (pebbles, bark, leaves, pine needles, pine
cones, nuts, seeds, wood shavings, shells, and dried flowers)
Aluminum pie pan
Heavy string or shoelace
Water

Have your child arrange the natural objects in the pie pan.
Fold the string in half and lay it in the pan so the fold is over
the edge and the two ends are in the center of the pan. Fill
the pan with water. If the weather is cold enough, place the
pan outside to freeze. If not, place it in your freezer. When
the water is frozen, remove the ice from the pan and hang it
outside.

Sun Painting

Dark-colored construction paper
Natural objects (leaves, twigs, pine cones, and so on) or
  household objects (scissors, keys, combs, and so on)

Place the paper outside in direct sunlight. Have your child arrange the objects on the paper, then leave them for a couple of hours. Remove the objects to see what the sun has painted.

Seedy Sponge

Natural sponge
Water
Heavy string
Birdseed

Soak the sponge in water, then tie the string around its middle. Have your child roll the sponge in birdseed, then hang the sponge in a sunny window for a few days and watch the seeds sprout.

Bleached Leaf Prints

Make sure your child wears old clothes for this project.

Newspaper
Leaves
Bleach
Shallow container
Clothespin
Cotton ball
Black construction paper

Cover your work surface with newspaper. Place the leaves vein side up on the newspaper. Pour a small amount of bleach into the container. Clip a clothespin onto a cotton ball and dip the cotton into the bleach. Have your child dab the bleach onto the leaf, then turn the leaf over and press it onto the black construction paper. Gently rub the leaf, then lift it off the paper to see the print it's left.

Weaving Wall

Hammer and nails
Chicken wire
Duct tape
Natural objects like wild grasses, flowers, and twigs
Weaving materials like yarn, ribbon, string, and shoelaces
  (optional)

Nail chicken wire along a fence or between two trees. Be sure to cover any sharp edges with duct tape. Encourage your child to weave natural objects through the wire. If you like, weave other materials through the wall.

Nature Colors

Plant life (grass, leaves, dandelions, and so on)
Crayons
Paper

Go on a walk with your child and bring home a variety of plant life. Spread your finds out on a table in your back yard and encourage your child to draw a picture using only crayons in colors that match the items you've collected.

Plaster Nature Art

2 cups water
Bucket
3 cups plaster of Paris
Paint stick or wooden spoon
Shallow box, old baking pan, or Styrofoam food tray
Natural objects (pebbles, bark, leaves, pine needles, pine
  cones, nuts, seeds, wood shavings, shells, and dried flowers)
Paintbrush and acrylic paints (optional)
Clear acrylic spray (optional)

Pour the water into the bucket. Sprinkle the plaster of Paris over the water and stir the mixture until it's about as thick as pea soup. Pour a layer of plaster into the bottom of the box, pan, or tray. Have your child arrange the natural objects in the plaster, then wait 10–20 minutes for the plaster to harden.

Carefully remove the plaster from the container. If you like, have your child paint the plaster, then spray it with clear acrylic spray when the paint is dry.

CHAPTER 8
Edible Arts and Crafts

The potential possibilities of any child are the most intriguing and stimulating in all creation.

—*Ray L. Wilbur*

Kitchens contain an array of ingredients for making creative, delicious arts and crafts. And since most kids love to create, eat, and be with their parents, making edible arts and crafts is a fun and constructive way to spend time together.

Kitchen activities also help young children develop hand-eye coordination, small motor skills, and reading and math skills, to name a few. Plus, learning to prepare food for themselves and others boosts young children's self-esteem and gives them skills they can use all their lives.

Most arts and crafts activities for young children should focus on the process rather than the product. But if you and your child want to eat your creations, directions must be followed, ingredients must be measured precisely, and so on. Creativity comes in when the dough is shaped or the cookies are painted.

Always be safety conscious. Make sure any dangerous kitchen objects are well out of your child's reach, and make a rule that only an adult can use sharp utensils, the oven, or the stove.

Alphabet Cookies

This special vanilla dough handles like modeling clay, but it also makes delicious cookies. Use this activity to strengthen your child's alphabet skills, to make place cards for children's birthday parties, or just to make a delicious treat.

4½ cups unsifted all-purpose flour
1½ cups butter
3 hard-boiled egg yolks
¾ cup sugar
3 raw egg yolks
1½ teaspoon vanilla extract
Colored sugar or chocolate chips (optional)

1. Preheat your oven to 300°F.
2. Measure the flour into a large bowl.
3. Cut the butter into small pieces and add them to the flour. Have your child mix the flour and butter with his hands until the mixture forms fine crumbs.
4. In a separate bowl, mash the hard-boiled egg yolks with the sugar. Stir this mixture into the flour mixture.
5. In a separate bowl, blend the raw egg yolks with the vanilla. Stir this mixture into the flour mixture with a fork.
6. Have your child press the mixture into a firm ball. Cover and refrigerate it if you plan to shape and bake it later. Otherwise, work with it at room temperature.

7. Roll out the dough. Cut 3- or 4-inch strips and have your child roll them with his hands to make ropes.
8. Shape the ropes into the letters of your child's name. Flatten them slightly so they're about ¼ inch thick. If you like, decorate them with colored sugar or chocolate chips.
9. Bake the letters on a baking sheet for 25–30 minutes.

Edible Mud Shapes

1 cup peanut butter
¼ cup honey
½ cup dry milk
1 cup crushed graham
  crackers
Chocolate milk powder

Rolling pin and cookie cutters
Raisins, chocolate chips,
  small candy pieces, or
  cookie decorations
  (optional)

1. Mix the peanut butter, honey, and dry milk in a medium bowl. Stir in the crushed graham crackers.
2. Use this mixture in one or more of the following ways:

   • Show your child how to form the mixture into balls. Pour a small amount of chocolate milk powder onto a plate and roll the balls in it. Or pour the powder into a Ziploc bag, add the balls, and shake to coat them.
   • Have your child roll the mixture with a rolling pin. Use cookie cutters or a small plastic knife to cut out shapes. If you like, decorate them with raisins, chocolate chips, small candy pieces, or cookie decorations.
   • Have your child create sculptures with the mixture. If you like, decorate them with raisins, chocolate chips, small candy pieces, or cookie decorations.
   • Have your child roll the dough into long ropes, then use the ropes to form letters, numbers, shapes, and so on.

Fruit Shapes

Watermelon or peeled apple
Knife
Small metal cookie cutters

1. Cut a watermelon or peeled apple into thin slices.
2. Give your child small metal cookie cutters and let him cut out shapes from the slices, then eat the shapes.

Grape Surprise

½ cup peanut butter
½ cup nonfat dry milk
2 tablespoons honey
Grapes

1. Mix the peanut butter, dry milk, and honey in a small bowl until a soft dough is formed.
2. Form the dough into 1-inch balls. Flatten the balls into circles about 2 inches in diameter.
3. Have your child place a grape in the center of each circle. Wrap the dough around each grape and pinch to seal.
4. Eat the treats or refrigerate and serve them later. This recipe makes 8–10 treats.

Popcorn Animals

¾ cup sugar
1 teaspoon white vinegar
¾ cup brown sugar
½ cup light corn syrup
½ cup water
¼ teaspoon salt
¾ cup butter
8 cups popped popcorn

1. Stir all the ingredients except the butter and popcorn in a pan over medium heat until the mixture is 260°F as measured with a candy thermometer.
2. Reduce the heat to low, then add the butter. Stir the mixture until the butter is melted.
3. Put the popcorn in a large bowl and pour the liquid over it. Let the mixture cool slightly.
4. Butter your child's hands and let him mold the popcorn into animal shapes.
5. Place the shapes on wax paper until they cool and harden.

Ice Cream Cone Clowns

Ice cream
Paper cupcake liners
Ice cream cones
Chocolate chips, raisins, nuts, candy, or other small edible
*   items*

1. Place a scoop of ice cream in each paper cupcake liner.
2. Place an ice cream cone upside down on top of each ice cream scoop.
3. Have your child make a face for each clown with chocolate chips, raisins, nuts, candy, or other small edible items.

Peanut Butter Pudding Paint

This activity may not be suitable before a meal, because the paint probably will be eaten up!

¼ cup dry milk
¼ cup instant vanilla pudding mix (about half a package)
⅔ cup water
2 tablespoons fresh peanut butter
Prepared pudding or individual-size container of pudding in
   any flavor (optional)

1. Measure the dry milk and pudding mix into a small bowl.
2. Add the water and stir for about 1½ minutes, using a small whisk.
3. Add the peanut butter and whisk the mixture until it's smooth.
4. Have your child use the pudding to finger paint on a tabletop, highchair tray, plastic or paper plate, or other smooth surface.

If you like, prepare any flavor of pudding ahead of time to use as finger paint, or use an individual-size container of prepared pudding.

Peanut Butter Play Dough

2 cups peanut butter
6 tablespoons honey
Dry milk
Cocoa powder (optional)
Edible decorations (chocolate chips, raisins, candy sprinkles,
and colored sugar)

1. Mix the peanut butter and honey in a bowl, adding dry milk gradually until the mixture has the consistency of bread dough.
2. Add cocoa powder if you like.
3. Turn the dough onto wax paper and have your child shape the dough, decorate it with edible treats, and eat it!

Finger Gelatin Fun

3 packets unflavored gelatin
One 12-ounce can frozen juice concentrate, thawed
1½ cups water

1. Mix the gelatin and the juice in a bowl. Bring the water to a boil in a medium saucepan.
2. Stir the gelatin/juice mixture into the boiling water until the gelatin dissolves.
3. Use the mixture in one of the following ways:

   • Pour the mixture into a lightly greased shallow pan and refrigerate it until it sets (about 2 hours). Help your child cut the gelatin with cookie cutters, or use a knife.
   • Pour the mixture into a lightly greased ice cube tray, small glasses, or other molds to create building blocks of various shapes and sizes. When the gelatin is set, have your child combine the shapes to create a wiggly building or sculpture.

If you don't have gelatin on hand, you can make finger gelatin by combining 12 ounces of Jell-O mix with 2½ cups boiling water.

Jellybean Picture

Ornamental Frosting (See Appendix A.)
Piece of cardboard covered with aluminum foil
Jellybeans

1. Spread the frosting on the aluminum foil.
2. Have your child arrange the jellybeans on the frosting to create a picture or design. He can eat his design later if he likes.
3. Use this project as a seasonal activity—use pastel jellybeans at Easter, green and red jellybeans at Christmas, and so on.

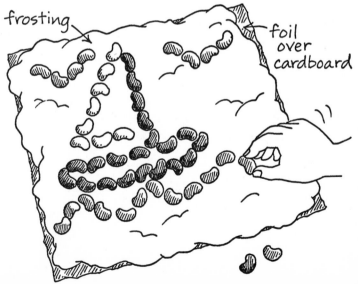

frosting

foil over cardboard

Painted Cookies

You can bake and glaze these sturdy cookies ahead of time, then paint them with food coloring on a rainy day or as a party project.

2 cups softened butter or margarine
2 cups granulated sugar
2 teaspoons vanilla extract
5 cups flour
6 cups powdered sugar
5–9 teaspoons warm water
Food coloring

1. Preheat your oven to 300°F.
2. Beat the butter, granulated sugar, and vanilla together in a large bowl.
3. Add the flour and mix the dough until it's thoroughly blended.
4. Roll out the dough until it's ¼–⅜ inch thick. Cut out cookies with a floured knife or cookie cutter.

5. Bake the cookies on an ungreased baking sheet for 25–30 minutes or until they're light golden brown. Let them cool for about 7 minutes, then transfer them to aluminum foil.

6. To make the glaze, pour the powdered sugar into a large bowl, then gradually stir in the warm water until the mixture is smooth and thick. Glaze the cookies and let them dry thoroughly (8–24 hours) before covering or moving them.

7. If you'll be painting the cookies later, store them at room temperature for up to 4 days. Freeze them for longer storage and thaw them before painting.

8. Paint the cookies with a clean paintbrush and small cups of undiluted food coloring for bright colors or slightly diluted food coloring for lighter colors. Food coloring will run, so let each color dry briefly before adding the next.

Nibbly Necklace

6 feet strong thread or embroidery floss
Large-eye needle
Cereal with holes, dry fruit, or soft candy like gumdrops

1. Thread the thread or floss through the needle, then slide the needle down so it's in the middle of the length of thread. Knot the ends together so the thread is doubled.
2. Help your child string cereal with holes, dry fruit, or soft candy onto the thread.
3. When the creation is long enough to fit over your child's head, cut the thread near the needle and knot the ends together to form a necklace he can nibble on.

Spider Crackers

Spread (cream cheese, cheese spread, or peanut butter)
Round crackers
Pretzel sticks
Raisins or chocolate chips

1. Smear the spread on two crackers.
2. Arrange eight pretzel sticks to look like spider legs in the spread on one of the crackers.
3. Place the second cracker spread side down on top of the first.
4. Have your child place two dots of spread on the top cracker, then top with two raisins or chocolate chips for spider eyes.

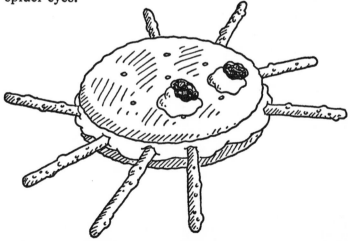

Crispy Rice Treats

¼ cup margarine or butter
4 cups miniature marshmallows or 40 large marshmallows
5 cups crispy rice cereal
Metal cookie cutters

1. Melt the margarine in a large saucepan.
2. Add the marshmallows and stir the mixture constantly over low heat until it's syrupy.
3. Remove the saucepan from the stove. Add the cereal and stir until it's well coated.
4. Use the mixture in one of the following ways:

   - Press the mixture into a baking pan and let it cool. Help your child use metal cookie cutters to cut out some treats.
   - Have your child use his hands to mold the mixture into shapes.

Snail Shells

Precise quantities aren't important in this recipe. Just use whatever's on hand!

Pastry dough scraps or ready-made pie, bread, or biscuit
  dough, thawed
Margarine or butter, softened
Brown sugar
Ground cinnamon

1. Preheat your oven to 350°F.
2. Roll the pastry into a rectangle about ⅛ inch thick. (Roll bread or biscuit dough slightly thicker.) The short sides of the rectangle should be at least 6 inches long.
3. Spread a thin layer of margarine over the dough.
4. Have your child sprinkle the dough with brown sugar and cinnamon.
5. Starting at a long side of the rectangle, roll up the dough tightly.
6. Cut the roll into ½-inch slices with a sharp knife. The slices will look like snail shells.
7. Lay the snail shells flat on a greased baking sheet, about 1 inch apart, and bake them for 10–15 minutes.
8. Transfer the snail shells to a wire rack to cool before eating them.

Pastry Cookies

1 package prepared piecrusts
Cookie cutters
½ cup sugar
2 tablespoons ground cinnamon

1. Preheat your oven to 450°F.
2. Unfold the piecrusts on wax paper. Have your child cut shapes from the piecrusts with the cookie cutters. (Or help him use a small plastic knife to cut letters, numbers, and shapes from the pastry.)
3. Mix the sugar and cinnamon in a small bowl and sprinkle the mixture over the cookies.
4. Place the cookies on an ungreased baking sheet and bake them for 8–10 minutes.
5. Transfer the cookies to a wire rack to cool before you eat them.

Alphabet Crackers

*Spread (peanut butter, jam, honey, cheese spread, cream
    cheese, Nutella, and so on)*
Crackers
Alphabet cereal

1. Smear spread on the crackers.
2. Help an older preschooler spell his name or a simple sentence like *I love you* by sticking alphabet cereal onto the crackers. A younger child may enjoy simply sticking the letters onto the crackers in no particular order.
3. Let your child eat his creations.

Gingerbread Critters

1 cup shortening
¾ cup honey
1 egg
1 cup molasses
1½ teaspoon baking soda
½ teaspoon salt
2 teaspoons ground ginger

1 teaspoon ground cinnamon
1 teaspoon ground cloves
5 cups flour
Animal-shaped cookie
  cutters
Raisins, nuts, licorice, and
  small candies for decorating

1. Preheat your oven to 375°F.
2. Mix the shortening, honey, egg, and molasses in a small bowl. Sift the baking soda, salt, ginger, cinnamon, cloves, and flour together into a large bowl.
3. Add the wet mixture to the dry one and mix well. Refrigerate the dough until it's chilled.
4. Roll out the dough on a floured surface until it's ¼ inch thick. Cut out shapes using animal-shaped cookie cutters and place the shapes onto an ungreased baking sheet.
5. Have your child decorate each shape with raisins, nuts, licorice, and other small candies. (Or bake the gingerbread critters ahead of time and let your child decorate the cooled cookies with frosting and small candies.)
6. Bake the animal shapes for 10 minutes and cool them before eating them.

Colorful Cookies

2 cups flour
½ teaspoon baking soda
Pinch of salt
1 cup sugar
½ cup butter

1 egg
2 teaspoons vanilla extract
1 teaspoon milk
Food coloring in a least
    2 colors

1. Mix the flour, baking soda, and salt in a medium bowl. Beat the sugar and butter in a large bowl.
2. Add the egg, vanilla, and milk to the sugar/butter mixture. Beat the mixture until it's light and creamy.
3. Add the flour mixture and mix the dough with your hands until it's smooth. Divide the dough into 2 equal halves.
4. Divide one half into 3 equal portions. Tint each portion a different color (one portion may remain uncolored, if desired). Mix in the food coloring well.
5. Roll each portion of dough into a log about ½ inch in diameter and 7 inches long. Gently roll the logs together to make a log about 1½ inches in diameter and 7 inches long.
6. Repeat steps 4–5 for the other half of dough.
7. Wrap each log in plastic wrap and freeze for 30 minutes or until the dough is firm enough to slice.
8. Preheat your oven to 400°F. Have your child use a Popsicle stick or plastic knife to cut the logs into ¼-inch slices and place them on a baking sheet.
9. Bake the cookies for 8–10 minutes. This recipe makes about 50 cookies.

Painted Eggs

Condensed-Milk Paint (See Appendix A.)
Small plastic container
Hard-boiled eggs

1. Pour a small amount of paint into the container. Use just one color to start, or use several colors at once.
2. Place a hard-boiled egg in the container and show your child how to gently tip the container from side to side to cover the egg with the paint.
3. Let the egg dry on a wire rack. Refrigerate the eggs you intend to eat.

Edible Edifice

*Spread (cheese spread, peanut butter, cottage cheese, cream
   cheese, jam, honey, and so on)*
Crackers
Cereal
Celery sticks
Apple slices
Raisins, nuts, and/or sunflower seeds

Put the spread on a small plate or in a small plastic container. Have your child use a small plastic knife or Popsicle stick to work with it in the following activities:

• Smear the spread onto a cracker, then stick another cracker on top of it. Continue building layers until the structure is complete. Use different kinds of crackers and/or cereal, if you like.
• Smear the spread onto celery sticks or apple slices. Top with raisins, nuts, and/or sunflower seeds.
• Use a combination of all the ingredients to form sculptures.

Bread Sculptures

1 cup warm water　　　*3–4 cups flour*
1 teaspoon sugar　　　*1 tablespoon vegetable oil*
1 package active dry yeast　*1 teaspoon salt*

1. Measure the water and sugar into a large bowl. Stir until the sugar is almost dissolved, then sprinkle the yeast into the water. Let the mixture sit for 10 minutes.
2. Add 1 cup of flour to the mixture and mix until smooth. Add the oil, salt, and another cup of flour to the dough and mix well.
3. Turn the dough onto a floured surface and knead it, adding flour as you knead until the dough is smooth and satiny. Place the dough in a greased bowl and cover with a clean dishtowel. Set the bowl in a warm place and let the dough rise for about 45 minutes.
4. Preheat your oven to 350°F.
5. Punch the dough down and knead it until smooth. Divide the dough into small portions and let your child shape or sculpt each portion as desired.
6. Place the dough sculptures on a greased baking sheet. Bake them for 15–20 minutes or until golden brown and firm.

If you like, thaw frozen bread dough and form shapes with it. Place the shapes onto a baking sheet and let them stand about 20 minutes. Bake them at 350°F or until golden brown.

Peanut Butter Logs

⅓ cup peanut butter
3 tablespoons honey
½ cup crushed corn flake cereal
½ cup quick-cooking oats
¼ cup dry milk
Chocolate sprinkles or colored sugar

1. Combine the peanut butter and honey in a medium bowl.
2. Add the cereal, oats, and dry milk. Mix well.
3. Place the chocolate sprinkles or colored sugar on a baking sheet.
4. Show your child how to roll a small portion of the dough into a log shape, then roll it in the sprinkles or sugar.
5. Repeat step 4 to make additional logs. If you like, stack the logs to form a building, or simply enjoy them as a delicious snack.

Pretzels

1¼ cups warm water
1½ teaspoons sugar
1 package active dry yeast
¼ teaspoon salt
4 cups flour
1 egg, beaten

1. Preheat your oven to 400°F.
2. Measure the water and sugar into a large bowl. Stir until the sugar is almost dissolved, then sprinkle the yeast into the water. Let the mixture sit for about 10 minutes.
3. Add the salt and flour to the mixture and mix until the dough forms a ball. Knead on a floured surface until the dough is smooth.
4. Cut the dough into small pieces, or pull off enough dough to form balls about 1½ inches in diameter. Help your child roll the balls into ropes about 12 inches long.
5. Twist the dough ropes into pretzel shapes and place them on a greased baking sheet.
6. Brush the pretzels with beaten egg and bake them for 15 minutes or until golden brown.

Zoo Sandwiches

Animal-shaped cookie cutters
Cheese slices
Bread

1. Use the cookie cutters to cut animal shapes from cheese slices.
2. Have your child place the animal shapes on slices of bread. Eat your zoo sandwiches!

Animal Snacks

Honey, peanut butter, or cream cheese
Graham crackers
Animal crackers

1. Spread honey, peanut butter, or cream cheese on graham crackers.
2. Have your child stand animal crackers upright in the spread. Eat your animal snacks!

Chocolate Chip Cookie Cake

1 cup margarine at room
  temperature
1 cup brown sugar, packed
1 cup granulated sugar
2 eggs, lightly beaten
2 tablespoons milk
2 teaspoons vanilla extract
2 cups sifted all-purpose
  flour
1 teaspoon baking powder
1 teaspoon baking soda
1 teaspoon salt
2 cups quick-cooking oats

1 cup (or more) chocolate
  chips
1 cup coarsely chopped
  walnuts
Rolling pin
Variety of circular shapes
  for tracing (approximately
  2 to 9 inches in diameter)
Plastic or table knife
Frosting
Candies for decorating
Birthday candle (optional)

1. Cream the margarine and sugars in a large bowl until light and fluffy.
2. Add the eggs, milk, and vanilla and beat the mixture until blended.
3. Sift the flour, baking powder, baking soda, and salt together in a separate bowl. Add the dry mixture to the wet one and stir the mixture just until it's blended.
4. Stir in the oats, then fold in the chocolate chips and walnuts.

5. Cover the dough and refrigerate it for at least 1 hour.
6. Preheat your oven to 350°F. Grease one or more baking sheets.
7. Roll the dough on a floured surface until it's ¼ inch thick. If necessary, add more flour.
8. Help your child use the circular shapes to trace and cut circles from the dough. (The number of circles will depend on how many layers you want your cake to have.) If you like, cut a small hole in the smallest circle to hold a birthday candle.
9. Transfer the circles to the baking sheets and bake them for 8–10 minutes or until golden brown.
10. When the cookie circles are cool, place the largest circle on a serving plate. Frost with a thin layer of frosting, then place the next largest circle on top. Repeat until all the cookie circles are stacked.
11. If you like, have your child decorate the cake with candies and additional frosting. If you like, place a birthday candle in the top of the cake.

If you like, substitute your own cookie dough for the cookie dough recipe in this activity. Try sugar cookies, gingerbread, shortbread, or whatever cookies you prefer.

Graham Cracker Gift Box

Graham crackers
Cardboard milk carton
Ornamental Frosting (See Appendix A.)
Edible decorations (gumdrops, raisins, chocolate chips, hard
  candies, and cereal)
Clear cellophane (optional)

1. Cut off the top of a cardboard milk carton so what's left is the same height as a graham cracker.
2. Use the frosting to stick graham crackers to the sides of the milk carton. Remember to cover the frosting with a damp cloth when you're not using it.
3. Have your child use additional frosting and edible decorations to decorate the gift box.
4. When the frosting is dry, place wrapped candies or a small gift inside. If you like, wrap the gift box with clear cellophane.

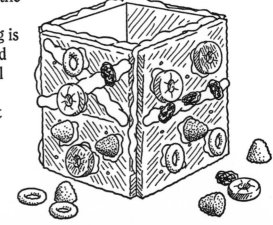

Edible Shapes

Variety of snack items (cheese slices, pretzel sticks, cereal,
  raisins, and so on)
Plastic knife
Pencil and paper

1. Place the snack items on a flat surface.
2. Challenge your child to make shapes with the snack
   items. He can fold or cut cheese slices to form triangles,
   line up pretzel sticks to make squares and rectangles, and
   arrange cereal and raisins into circles.
3. If you like, draw the outline of several shapes on paper.
   Show your child how to arrange the snack items on top
   of the outlines to form the shapes.

Potato Sculptures

Mashed potatoes   *Melted butter or margarine*
Baking sheet

1. Preheat your oven to 350°F.
2. Encourage your child to shape the potatoes into sculptures.
3. Place the sculptures on a baking sheet and brush them
   with melted butter.
4. Bake the sculptures for 10–15 minutes.

Puffed Wheat Treats

This recipe requires boiling a syrupy mixture on the stove, so please use caution when young children are near.

½ cup margarine
⅔ cup corn syrup
1 cup brown sugar

2 tablespoons cocoa powder
(optional)
1 teaspoon vanilla extract
8 cups puffed wheat

1. Melt the margarine in a heavy saucepan. Stir in the corn syrup, brown sugar, and cocoa powder if desired.
2. Bring the mixture to a boil over medium-high heat, stirring constantly. Boil for one minute, then remove the pan from the heat.
3. Stir in the vanilla.
4. Measure the puffed wheat into a large bowl.
5. Add the hot syrup mixture to the puffed wheat and mix well.
6. Use the mixture in one of the following ways:

   - Allow the mixture to cool slightly, then have your child use his hands to mold it into sculptures.
   - Press the mixture onto a greased baking sheet. Let the mixture cool, then help your child cut shapes from it with cookie cutters.

Colorful Cubes

*Beverages in a variety of colors (purple grape juice, blue
  Kool-Aid, pink lemonade, red cranberry juice, and so on)
Ice cube trays
Clear drinking glasses
Small Ziploc bags (optional)*

1. Pour the beverages into ice cube trays and place them in your freezer.
2. When the ice cubes are frozen, let your child have fun experimenting with them. Have him see how a glass of lemonade changes color when a purple ice cube is placed in it. Or how blue ice cubes change the color of a glass of cranberry juice.
3. If you like, let your child combine cubes of different colors in small Ziploc bags and observe what color appears when the cubes melt.

Candy Sculptures

⅓ cup butter, softened
⅓ cup light corn syrup
½ teaspoon salt

1 teaspoon flavor extract of
 your choice
4 cups powdered sugar
Food coloring

1. Let your child mix all the ingredients but the food color-
    ing in a large bowl with a wooden spoon until the dough
    becomes stiff, then knead it until it's smooth.
2. Divide the dough into several portions and put each in a
    separate container. Add a few drops of food coloring to
    each container and mix well.
3. Have your child create designs and sculptures with the
    candy mixture. Let him combine the colors, if he likes.
    Or to make candies, have your child
    roll spoonfuls of dough into balls and
    flatten them lightly with a fork.
4. Place the sculptures or candies on a
    baking sheet lined with wax paper
    and refrigerate them for 30
    minutes or until they're
    firm. Store them covered
    in the refrigerator.

Biscuit Shapes

2 cups all-purpose flour
1 tablespoon baking powder
1 teaspoon salt
¼ cup butter or margarine
¾ cup milk
Orange juice
Sugar cubes

1. Preheat your oven to 450°F.
2. Have your child mix the flour, baking powder, and salt in a large bowl with a fork.
3. With a pastry blender or 2 knives used scissor-fashion, cut in the butter until the mixture resembles coarse crumbs.
4. Add the milk. With a fork, quickly mix the mixture just until it forms a soft dough.
5. Knead in extra flour if necessary to make the dough workable.
6. Roll the dough on a floured surface until it's ½ inch thick. Cut shapes from it with cookie cutters or a plastic or table knife. Place the shapes on an ungreased baking sheet.
7. Show your child how to quickly dip a sugar cube into orange juice, then press it into the top of a biscuit. Repeat this step for the remaining biscuits.
8. Bake the biscuits for 12–15 minutes or until they're golden brown.
9. Serve them with butter and/or jam. This recipe makes about 12 biscuits.

Consumable Collage

Peanut butter or Ornamental Frosting (See Appendix A.)
Piece of cardboard covered with aluminum foil
Variety of snack items (pretzels, cereal, animal crackers,
   Goldfish crackers, chocolate chips, raisins, licorice, candy
   pieces, and so on)

1. Spread the peanut butter or Ornamental Frosting on the
   aluminum foil.
2. Have your child arrange a variety of snack items in the
   peanut butter or frosting to create a picture or design.
3. When the collage is complete, you may like to take a
   photo of it before you eat it.

CHAPTER 9
Educational Arts and Crafts

Imagination is more important than knowledge.
—Albert Einstein

Because children learn through their senses, arts and crafts projects are ideal for learning. Children see how a new color forms when two colors of paint are combined, or they feel how sand glued onto a picture changes its texture.

The following activities are some creative, fun ways to help your child develop skills like sorting, matching, classifying, and recognizing patterns, shapes, colors, and so on—skills required to learn basic math and reading skills.

All parents want their children to succeed, but you must not push academics. Children must spend their early years developing the large and small motor skills that make learning possible and productive. Provide a stimulating environment for your child. Limit passive activities like watching TV, and give her lots of free time to be creative and use her imagination. Read to her each day and let her see you reading for pleasure. And don't approach the following activities any differently than you would other activities you do together. Just have fun!

Shiny Shapes

Construction paper
Pencil or marker
Paint pens
Glue
Cotton swab (optional)
Glitter or Colorful Creative Salt (See Appendix A.)
Paintbrush and Puffy Paint or Crystal Paint (See Appendix A.)
Scissors, hole punch, and string or ribbon (optional)

Draw various shapes (square, rectangle, triangle, heart, circle, oval, star, and so on) on the paper. Have your child finish the shapes in one of the following ways:

- Use paint pens, which leave raised lines when dry, to outline and decorate each shape.
- Squeeze glue or use a cotton swab to spread glue onto the outlines. Sprinkle glitter or Colorful Creative Salt over the shapes. Tip off the extra glitter or salt and practice saying the name of each shape.
- Paint each shape with Puffy Paint or Crystal Paint.

If you like, make each shape a hanging ornament. Cut out each shape and punch a hole near the top edge. Thread string or ribbon through the hole and tie the ends securely.

Shape Painting

Liquid tempera paint(s)
Shallow container(s)
Paper cups, small jars, Duplo blocks, sponges, and other
objects in different geometric shapes
Several sheets of paper

Pour liquid tempera paint into a shallow container. If you like, use more than one color, using one container for each color.

Collect assorted objects in basic geometric shapes. Help your child dip the objects into the paint, then press them onto the paper. You may wish to use one sheet of paper for each shape, or use one sheet of paper for all the shapes, each a different color.

If possible, use each object in more than one way. For example, a cup may leave a faint outline of a circle if pressed onto the paper upside down, but its base may leave a solid circle. A Duplo block will leave either a row of small circles or a larger square or rectangle, depending on which side is pressed on the paper.

Tracing Collage

Scissors
Heavy paper or thin cardboard
Construction paper
Colored marker(s)

Cut basic geometric shapes (circle, square, rectangle, and triangle) from the paper or cardboard. Have your child select a shape and trace around it on the construction paper with a marker. Move the shape, then trace again. Keep moving the shape and tracing until you have many overlapping outlines of the same shape. If you like, change markers to make a colorful shape collage. If you like, change shapes so you have a variety of shapes on one collage.

Tactile Letters

Feeling the alphabet shapes helps some kids learn the letters of the alphabet.

Pencil
Construction paper
Cotton swab or paintbrush
Glue
Sand or Colorful Creative Salt (See Appendix A.)

Lightly pencil the outline of one or more letter shapes on the paper. Have your child trace the shape(s) with a cotton swab that's been dipped in glue, or squeeze glue onto each outline directly from the bottle. Sprinkle sand over the paper, then shake it lightly to remove any excess. Allow the glue to dry.

- Have your child trace the letter shape with her finger and say its name.
- Have her close her eyes, feel the shape, and try to identify the letter.
- Have your child trace the letter shape with her finger, then close her eyes and draw the letter shape with her finger on a table or other flat surface.

Triangle Fun

Drinking straws, toothpicks, Popsicle sticks, wooden skew-
ers, and other straight objects
Glue (optional)
Cardboard or heavy paper (optional)

Have your child use assorted straight objects to create triangles. If you like, glue the triangles onto cardboard or
heavy paper to create a triangle collage.

Button Board

Glue gun
Buttons
12-inch square of heavy cardboard
Shoelace or length of yarn

Help an older child use a glue gun to glue buttons onto the
heavy cardboard. When the glue is dry, have your child wrap
a shoelace or yarn around the buttons to create designs. Ask
her to try to create various shapes like a triangle, rectangle,
star, and so on. If you like, use buttons in just three colors,
perhaps red, blue, and yellow. Ask your child to wrap the
shoelace around only red buttons, or only blue buttons,
and so on.

3-D Number Board

Marker
Ruler
Heavy cardboard (at least 8½-by-11 inches)
Small objects like beads, buttons, paper clips, dry pasta,
  cereal, coins, toothpicks, and so on
Glue

Use a marker and ruler to divide the cardboard into 12 rows.
In the top row, write a title like "I Can Count!" or "Sam's
Numbers." Along the left edge of the cardboard, below the
title row, write one number in each row, beginning with 0
and ending with 10.

　　Help your child collect small objects in groups
of 1 to 10. Glue each group of objects
onto the appropriate row.
Display the poster
where your child
can touch each
object as she
counts it.

231

Play Dough Shapes

Broad-tip marker
Several sheets of construction paper or other colored paper
Clear contact paper
Play dough

Use a broad-tip marker to draw shapes (a circle, square, rectangle, triangle, oval, crescent, and so on) on the construction paper, one shape per sheet. Cover each sheet of paper with clear contact paper.

Have your child roll the play dough into ropes and shape them over each drawn shape. Then have her close her eyes, feel each play dough shape, and try to identify it.

If you like, draw letters and numbers on additional sheets of paper and repeat the process.

Button Collage

Marker
3 sheets of cardboard or
heavy paper

Assorted buttons
Glue

Write the numbers 1, 2, and 4 on separate sheets of cardboard. Have your child sort the buttons by the number of holes each has, placing buttons with one hole on the sheet marked 1, two-hole buttons on the sheet marked 2, and so on. When all the buttons have been sorted, use the glue to create one-hole, two-hole, and four-hole button collages.

Seed Count

Knife
Apple, orange, melon, or
other fruit with seeds

Tempera paint
Shallow container
Paper

Cut the fruit in half and remove all the seeds. Count the seeds with your child. Pour paint into the container. Have your child dip the fruit halves in the paint and press them on the paper to make prints of the fruit.

Number Book

Small notebook or sheets of paper stapled together
Crayons or markers
Glue
Scissors
Old magazines
Stickers
Camera and film, or photos (optional)

Help your child print a number from 0 to 10 (or higher) on each page of a small notebook. On each page, have your child draw the corresponding number of objects, glue the corresponding number of pictures (cut from old magazines), or stick on a corresponding number of stickers.

If you like, have your child help you find groups of objects around the home (for example, one doll, two toy cars, three balls, four books, and so on). Take a photo of each group of objects (or search through existing photos for groups of people or objects) and glue the photos into your number book.

Number Cards

22 small index cards
Black marker
Stickers or dot stickers

Help your child write the numbers from 0 to 10 on small index cards, writing one number in the center of each of two index cards. If you like, also write the words for each number: zero, one, two, and so on. Show her how to put one sticker on the index cards featuring the number 1, two stickers on the cards with the number 2, and so on. Place the cards faceup and have your child match all the pairs. Place the cards facedown and play a memory game, taking turns turning over one card then trying to turn over the matching one. If you make a match, you keep the pair. If not, turn the cards facedown for the next player's turn. The player with the most pairs wins the game.

Edible Pattern

This is another exercise to help your child practice sorting and counting.

Colorful cereal like Froot Loops
String or yarn
Tape measure (optional)

Pour some colorful cereal on a table or other work surface. Have your child group the cereal by color. Select two or more groups and arrange them in a pattern. You may want to simply alternate two colors, or arrange a more complex pattern.

Tie the first piece of cereal to string or yarn, then help your child add the rest of the cereal according to the pattern you've arranged. Repeat the pattern until the necklace is as long as you want it, then tie the ends together.

If you like, count how many pieces of cereal are on the string. Use a tape measure to measure the length of the necklace.

Pattern Play

Working with patterns is fun for kids and helps develop problem-solving abilities necessary for mathematical thinking.

Plain paper
Ruler
Pencil
Colored markers or crayons

On the paper, use the ruler and pencil to mark off a grid of squares, making an equal number of rows and columns. The number of squares in a row should be at least one more than the number of letters in your child's name. For example, a child named Mark calls for a grid that's at least 5 rows by 5 columns.

Have your child write her name in the top row, starting at the top left square and writing one letter in each square. When she completes her name, have her write it again, starting in the next square in the top row. When she comes to the end of the row, have her continue the name on the next row. Have her keep writing her name this way until all the squares are filled.

Have your child color the first letter of her name wherever it appears on the grid. Notice the pattern the colored squares make. If you like, color other letters in different colors and notice the patterns they make.

Painted Sticks

Paintbrushes
Popsicle sticks
Tempera or acrylic paints in assorted colors
Colored construction paper
Rubber bands

Let your child paint Popsicle sticks in assorted colors. When the sticks are dry, have her use them in the following ways:

- Mix up the sticks and sort them into piles by color.
- Lay out colored construction paper. Match the sticks to the paper by color.
- Count the sticks that have been sorted by color. Place the piles of sticks in order from fewest to most.
- Use rubber bands to group the sticks by twos, fives, and tens. Practice counting by twos, fives, and tens.

Four Seasons Poster

Poster board   *Scissors*
Marker   *Glue*
Old magazines   *Family photos (optional)*

Divide the poster board into four sections. Label each section with one of the four seasons. Help your child look through old magazines for pictures that depict seasonal elements and activities. Cut out the pictures and glue them onto the appropriate sections.

If you like, look through your photos and choose ones that depict your child or family in seasonal activities: swimming at the beach, admiring spring flowers, playing in the snow, and so on. Glue the photos into the appropriate sections.

If you like, create a "Day and Night" poster by dividing the poster board into two sections and gluing on magazine pictures or family photos that depict day and night activities.

Calendar Math

At the end of every month, help your child make a calendar for the coming month.

Poster board or large sheet of construction paper
Ruler
Markers
Stickers

On poster board, use a ruler and markers to make a calendar grid. Help your child label the calendar with the month and day names and write the day numbers in each square. Let your child decorate the calendar with seasonal images, and mark holidays, birthdays, and other special days with stickers or drawings.

Read the calendar with your child every day. Say the day, the date, the month, and the year. For example, you might say, "Today is Tuesday. That means yesterday was Monday, and tomorrow will be Wednesday. Today is the twenty-ninth of July 2003. That means yesterday was the twenty-eighth and tomorrow will be the thirtieth." Then let your child cross off each day, or place a sticker in the calendar square.

Telling Time

Scissors
Construction paper
Paper fastener
Paper plate
Crayon, pen, or marker

Cut hour and minute hands from the construction paper and attach them with a paper fastener to the center of a paper plate. Number the plate to look like a clock face. Use this play clock in the following activities:

- Encourage your child to move the hands around the clock as she learns the basics of telling time. (Most young children who can count to twelve can easily learn to tell time by the hour.)
- Have your child use the play clock to answer questions such as, "If it's six o'clock now, what time will it be in two hours?" and "If it's seven o'clock now and we ate dinner one hour ago, what time did we eat dinner?" and "If it's two o'clock now, how many hours until it's eight o'clock?"
- Set the play clock next to a standard (nondigital) clock. Set the time on the play clock to the starting time of an anticipated event like snack time or the start of a favorite TV show. Have your child compare the real clock with the play clock and let you know when they match.

Map Skills

Large sheet of paper
Pens or markers
Glue

Paints and paintbrushes,
*   sturdy cardboard or wood,*
*   and milk cartons or small*
*   boxes (optional)*

- Help your child draw a simple map of her neighborhood. Include familiar landmarks on her map: the mailbox, the store, the playground, her friend's house, the fire station. Take this map with you on your walks and point out the landmarks as you go. Collect small natural objects like acorns and leaves. At home, glue these objects onto the map where you found them.
- Draw maps of your yard, your house, or your child's bedroom.
- On a very large sheet of paper, draw an imaginary city big enough for your child's toy cars and trucks. Include familiar places like the bank, grocery store, gas station, park, school, church, post office, and so on. Let her color and decorate the city. Tape the finished city to the floor so your child can travel around the city with her cars, trucks, dolls, and fire engines. Or for a more permanent city, paint streets on sturdy cardboard or wood. Paint and decorate milk cartons or small boxes and glue them onto the map to make buildings.

First Words Scrapbook

Scissors
Old magazines
Glue
Scrapbook
Photos of family and friends
Permanent marker

Cut out magazine pictures of people, animals, and objects your child can identify. Help her glue them into a scrapbook. Include photos of family and friends. Use a permanent marker to label each picture and photo. Your child will enjoy looking at the pictures and eventually will learn to recognize some of the words, too.

Raisin Play

Raisins
Several toothpicks

Paper
Pen, crayon, or marker

Stick one raisin on the tip of each of several toothpicks.
Write large letters and/or shapes on the paper and challenge
your child to connect the toothpicks to create each letter
and/or shape. For older preschoolers, you may not need to
write the letters or shapes.

Keep in mind that your child will eat some of the raisins
(which makes the activity more fun), so keep plenty on hand.

Color Collage

Paint swatches in assorted
  colors and shades
Scissors

Construction paper
Glue

Collect assorted paint swatches from a home-improvement
store. Cut each in half. Mix up the pieces and have your child
sort and match shades. Arrange the pieces on construction
paper and glue them into place to create a colorful collage.

Ready to Read

The following ideas are adapted from the U.S. Department of Education booklet *Helping Your Child Become a Reader.*

Paper
Pencils, crayons, or markers
Blank notebook or scrapbook
Glue
Family photos or scissors and old magazines

- Use paper and pencils, crayons, or markers to make an alphabet poster with your child.
- Label the things drawn in your child's pictures. If your child draws a picture of a house, label it "house" and display the picture on the refrigerator.
- Have your child watch you write when you make shopping or to-do lists. Say the words out loud as you write them and carefully print each letter. Encourage your child to make lists, too. Help her form the letters and spell the words.
- Make a travel journal with your child. Each evening, write in a blank notebook or scrapbook about the day's special events. Later, glue in family photos or pictures cut from magazines that depict the events.

Letter Puzzles

Construction paper
Scissors
Glue

From the paper, cut rectangles ½ inch by 4 inches, rectangles ½ inch by 2 inches, circles with 4-inch diameters, and circles with 2-inch diameters. Cut some circles in half.

Show your child how to arrange the shapes on paper to form letters. Help her trim some of the shapes (for example, to form the curved ascender in the letter *f,* or the curved descender in the letter *j*). Glue the shapes into place to form letters and words.

"I Can" Scrapbook

Scrapbook
Samples of your child's artwork
Glue

As your child masters skills, add appropriate pages to a scrapbook. Glue in one of her paintings and label the page, "I Can Paint." Glue in other samples under titles like "I Can Color," "I Can Cut," "I Know Shapes," "I Can Count," and so on.

Personal Time Line

Paper
Markers
Scissors, tape, glue, and photos (optional)

A time line can be as short as one page or as long as a wall.

To make a short time line, draw a vertical line down the middle of a sheet of paper. Write your child's birth date on the left side of the line at the top of the page. On the right side of the line, write the corresponding event. ("I was born!") Add other important dates and events, like when your child started to walk and talk, when her siblings were born, when she started preschool, when you took family trips, and so on, in chronological order.

To make a long time line, cut a length of paper from a large roll or tape several sheets of paper together. Draw a horizontal line across the middle of the banner. Write the dates and events of your child's life from left to right. Let your child glue on photos or illustrate each event. Hang the time line in your child's room and add to it occasionally.

March 30, 1997 I was born	Dec. 1997 I started to walk	Sept. 2001 I went to school	Jan. 14, 2002 Susie was born	Summer 2002 trip to California	Sept. I st I st

Family Phone Book

Scissors
Paper
Photos of family and friends
Small photo album (sleeves each measuring at least
   4-by-6 inches)
Markers, crayons, or colored pencils

Cut the paper into 4-by-6-inch rectangles. Collect photos of
family and friends and insert them into the photo album,
leaving one blank sleeve between each photo. Have your
child write the name and telephone number of the person in
the first photo on one of the rectangles. Insert the rectangle
opposite the photo, next to it, or above or below it, depending
on the album's format. Repeat this process for each photo.

Alphabet Book

This is a good rainy day project that can be completed during one or more sittings.

Crayons or markers
Small notebook or sheets
of paper folded together
and stapled inside a
construction paper cover

Glue
Photos
Scissors
Old magazines

Help your child print a letter of the alphabet on each page of a small notebook. Use the alphabet book in one of the following ways:

- Have your child write words she knows on the appropriate pages: *cat* on the *C* page, *Mom* on the *M* page, and so on. She can illustrate the words or glue in appropriate photos or pictures cut from magazines.
- On each page, have your child draw a picture of an animal that begins with that letter, or cut animal pictures from old magazines and glue them onto the page.
- Look through magazines and grocery store fliers for pictures of food that begin with each letter of the alphabet. Cut out the pictures and glue them onto the appropriate pages. If you like, help your child label the pictures.

Personal Record Book

Children are naturally interested in themselves. Helping them collect and record personal information gives them the opportunity to develop reading, writing, and math skills.

Blank notebook or scrapbook
Pens or markers
Family photos
Glue
Tape measure
Stickers for decorating pages

Have your child create a title page on the first page of a notebook. She might include her photo, her full name, and the current date. Let her decorate the page with stickers. Include some or all of the following pages in the record book:

- **Address and telephone number page:** Glue a photo of your home onto the page, and write your address and telephone number under it, as well as other important phone numbers.
- **Family page:** Glue on this page photos of as many members of your immediate or extended family as you like.
- **Body measurements page:** Measure your child's height, arm span, and circumference of head and waist. Record the measurements on the page. Also include your child's weight, shoe size, temperature, pulse, and so on. If you

like, include a page for charting her height and weight over time. Older children may enjoy creating simple bar graphs to show height and weight changes over time.

- **Anniversary page:** From time to time, include a page that captures your child at a specific age. For example, every year on her birthday, include a page with her photo; a lock of hair; a record of age, height, weight, and shoe size; and so on. If you like, include a page depicting her likes and dislikes, friends, birthday celebrations, and so on.

Table Rubbings

Scissors
Heavy cardboard
Masking tape or poster putty (optional)
Large sheet of paper
Several crayons, papers removed

Cut geometric shapes, letters, and numbers from heavy cardboard (or buy them precut from an educational supply store). Arrange the cutouts randomly on a table, using some rolled-up masking tape or poster putty to hold them in place, if you like. Cover the table with the paper. Give your child several crayons. Show her how to rub the crayons sideways over the paper and see the shapes appear. If you like, move the paper and rub again. Have fun identifying the shapes, letters, and numbers. Display the paper or use it as gift-wrap.

CHAPTER 10
Toys, Gifts, and More

Every child must express himself every day, with words and music...with the picture he paints and the dolls he makes. Somehow he has to tell what's on his mind and he doesn't care if he has talent or not; it's what he says that counts.
—Marguerite Kelly and Elia Parsons

One problem that parents of young children often face is, "What shall we do with all these beautiful things our children create?" Only so many finger paintings can be displayed on the refrigerator, and shelves can quickly become cluttered with craft exhibits. One solution is to have your child do arts and crafts projects that serve a dual purpose—ones that provide creative experiences for him, but also make practical products or gifts.

The arts and crafts projects in this chapter focus on creating items that can be played with, worn, given away, or otherwise put to some practical use. And just because the product is practical doesn't make the project any less creative or fun to do. As Mary Mayesky, the widely respected author of *Creative Activities for Young Children* (Delmar Learning, 2001), writes, "The process of making something utilitarian, that can be used, does not negate the process or producing from being creative and artistic."

Musical Instruments

Your child will have fun using these homemade rhythm instruments to accompany his favorite music.

Several small items that make noise when shaken (dry beans, small dry pasta, popcorn kernels, pennies, and so on)
Paper plates
Glue or stapler
Hole punch
Ribbon
Crayons, markers, stickers, and other decorating items
Assortment of small containers
Blocks of wood
Paint and paintbrush
Sandpaper
Can opener
Empty coffee can and two plastic lids to cover the top and bottom rims
Paper
Unsharpened pencils or chopsticks

- Place the small items on a paper plate. Cover them with a second paper plate, then glue or staple the rims together. When the glue is dry, punch holes around the rims and lace ribbon through the holes. Let your child decorate the tambourine with crayons and so on.

- Help your child partially fill the assortment of small containers with the small items. Seal the containers, then shake them in time to your favorite music.
- Help your child decorate two blocks of wood with paint, markers, or stickers, then bang them together in time to a rhythmic beat.
- Glue sandpaper onto two blocks of wood, then rub them together for an interesting sound.
- Create a drum by using a can opener to cut the bottom out of an empty coffee can. If you like, have your child draw a picture on some paper and glue the paper around the can. Glue plastic lids on each end of the can. Use unsharpened pencils or chopsticks as drumsticks.

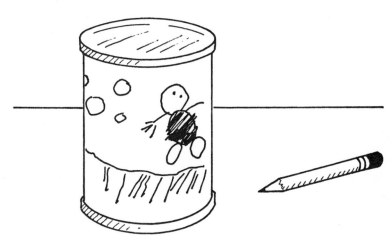

Creature Racers

Walnut shell halves   *Felt scraps*
Paint and paintbrush   *Markers*
Glue   *Marbles*
Googly eyes

Help your child decorate the shell halves to look like animals or creatures. Paint the shells, and glue on googly eyes, felt-scrap ears, legs, tails, and so on. Use a marker to draw on facial features.

Place each creature over a marble and race them along a flat surface.

Decorated Shoelaces

White shoelaces
Colorful permanent markers

Help your child decorate each shoelace with a bright pattern of dots, stripes, wavy lines, flowers, hearts, butterflies, or any other design you like. Draw with bold strokes, and don't hold the marker on the shoelace too long or the ink will soak through to the other side. Remember to decorate both sides of the shoelace.

Keepsake Book

Use this keepsake book to store special mementoes your child collects throughout the year.

Scissors
Cardboard
8–10 small Ziploc bags
Gift-wrap, markers, stickers, and so on
Glue
Hole punch
Ribbon

Cut 2 rectangles from the cardboard, each slightly larger than the Ziploc bags you're using. Have your child decorate each rectangle with gift-wrap and so on. Help your child write on 1 rectangle a title like "My Keepsake Book," "Nicole's Special Things," or "Things I Want to Save."

Stack the Ziploc bags and place them between the 2 rectangles (the one with the title on top). Arrange the bags so the openings are either along the top edge or the right edge. Punch 2 holes along the left edge of the bags and cardboard. Thread the ribbon through the holes and tie it in a bow on the front cover.

Stick Puppets

Popsicle sticks
Tape
Scissors
Photo of your child, family members, or friends
(head should be 1½–2 inches in diameter)
Construction paper
Glue
Fabric scraps

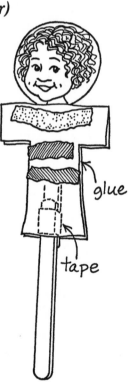

Tape 2 Popsicle sticks together end to
end, overlapping the ends for strength.
Cut a circle from the photo, about 1½–2
inches in diameter. (The circle should
include most of the head.) Tape the
back of the circle to one end of the
taped-together Popsicle sticks.

    Fold the paper in half. Cut a T shape
from it, making sure the fold is the top
of the T. Cut a small slit in the middle
of the fold and insert the Popsicle stick
through it. Glue the front and back of
the paper together. Have your child glue
on fabric scraps to dress the puppet.

Tie-Dyed Socks

White socks
Rubber bands
Old bucket
Old towels
8 cups cold water
4 cups hot water

Old bowl
Cold-water dye
Old wooden spoon
Cold dye fix
6 tablespoons salt

Wash the socks, then squeeze out the excess water. To make striped socks, wrap rubber bands at different intervals around the sock. To make circles, gather small bunches of the sock and wrap the bands 1 inch down from the tops of the bunches.

Place the bucket on a surface covered with an old towel. Pour the cold water into the bucket. Pour 2 cups of the hot water into the bowl. Stir the dye into the hot water. Pour the dye mixture into the bucket of cold water. Rinse the bowl.

Pour another 2 cups of hot water into the bowl. Use the spoon to stir in the cold dye fix and the salt until the salt dissolves. Stir this mixture into the bucket.

Have your child place the socks in the bucket and stir them slowly and gently for about 10 minutes. Leave the socks in the bucket for another 50 minutes, stirring occasionally.

Remove the socks from the dye and rinse them under cold running water until the water runs almost clear. Squeeze the socks and roll them in an old towel to remove excess water. Remove the rubber bands. Wash and dry the socks by themselves before they are worn.

Button Necklace

Large buttons (or construction paper, scissors, and hole
* punch)*
Shoelace, yarn, or ribbon

Give your child an assortment of large buttons, or cut circles
from construction paper and punch one, two, or four holes
in each circle. Show your child how to make a button necklace by threading the buttons onto a shoelace, yarn, or ribbon.

Handy Memories

This activity is great for a child's birthday party.

Piece of cardboard   *Paintbrushes*
T-shirt or pillowcase   *Camera and film (optional)*
Fabric paints

Insert the cardboard into the T-shirt so it lies flat. Paint the
palm sides of the children's hands (one or both) and press
them onto the fabric. Help the children who are able write
their names with fabric paint next to their handprints. Add a
caption like "Kelsey's Friends," "Chantal's 7th Birthday," or
"Grandma's Little Angels." If you like, take a group photo
that can be used as a transfer and ironed onto the shirt later.

Arty Apparel

Prewashed cotton sweatshirt or T-shirt
Piece of cardboard (optional)
Brightly colored crayons
Tape or stencils (optional)
Newspaper
Iron

Lay the sweatshirt on a hard, flat surface and tape it in place. Or, if you like, insert a piece of cardboard into the shirt so it lies flat. Encourage your child to color firmly on the fabric. If you like, use tape to make letters or numbers on the fabric, and have your child color around the edges. Your child may also enjoy using a stencil to color a shape onto the fabric. Remind your child to press firmly and use lots of color.

When the design is complete, remove any tape. Place the shirt colored side down on newspaper set on your ironing board. Iron the back of your design for a minute or so. Remove the newspaper, replace it with a fresh sheet, and iron the shirt again in the same way. Repeat this process until color no longer transfers to the newspaper.

Zipper Bracelets

Use your child's wrist to measure the length of a bracelet
for a child, and use your wrist to measure the length of a
bracelet for an adult.

One 6- or 7-inch zipper
Scissors
Velcro
Craft glue or glue gun
Small plastic jewels or beads
Fabric paint

Wrap the zipper around your or your child's wrist and note
where the ends overlap. Cut a strip of Velcro to fit the width
of the zipper and glue it onto the zipper where the ends
overlap, gluing one half of the strip to the correct side of the
zipper and the other half to the wrong side.

Help your child glue small jewels onto the
fabric part of the zipper.
Use fabric paint to make
designs or write names
or phrases around
the jewels.

Velcro

Magnetic Sign

Glue or glue gun
8-by-3-inch piece of cardboard
24 Popsicle sticks
Acrylic paints
Paintbrush
Broad-tip marker (optional)
Clear acrylic spray
Magnetic strip

Help your child spread glue on the cardboard and arrange the Popsicle sticks side by side across the width of the cardboard. Press on the sticks firmly, then let the glue dry.

Have your child paint the Popsicle sticks to create whatever kind of sign he wants. If you like, choose one of the painting processes described in Chapter 3. When the paint is dry, he may wish to use a marker to write his name or a message on the sign. Spray the sign with clear acrylic spray. Glue a magnetic strip onto the back of the sign and display it on your refrigerator, dishwasher, or other metal surface.

Painted Tile

Odds and ends of plain ceramic tile are great fun to paint.
You can hang painted tiles on a wall or use them for coasters
or trivets.

Acrylic paints
Paintbrushes, sponges, and/or small stickers
Plain ceramic tile
Clear acrylic spray
Glue gun (optional)
Marbles or wooden beads (optional)

Let your child paint on a plain piece of tile. He can paint a
design, scene, or message with paintbrushes; use sponges to
paint a colorful design; or stick stickers on the tile, paint
over them, and remove the stickers when the paint is dry.

When your child's masterpiece is finished, spray the tile
with clear acrylic spray. If your child has made a trivet, you
might also use a glue gun to glue marbles or wooden beads
to the underside of the tile (one in each corner).

Stringing Straw

Drinking straws in several colors
Scissors
Yarn or cord
Large tube-shaped dry pasta (optional)
Paint and paintbrushes (optional)

Have your child cut the drinking straws into various lengths.
Tie a large knot at the end of the yarn, then show your child
how to string on the straw pieces. (If using yarn and the end
frays, wrap a piece of tape tightly around the end or dip it in
glue to smooth the tip.) Your child may decide to create a
long length of straws to drape around his room, or he may
choose to make a necklace or other unique creation.

If you like, use large tube-shaped dry pasta that's been
painted first instead of straws. String on the pasta in a colorful pattern.

Layered Sand Art

Sand
Large shallow containers
Powdered tempera paint in several colors
Spoon
Glass jar or bottle with lid or cap

Pour sand into the containers and add a different color of paint to each container. Don't add paint to one container. Show your child how to color the sand by mixing it with the paint.

Choose one color of sand and pour a 1-inch layer of it into the jar. Change colors and add additional layers, varying the thickness of each layer. When the jar is full, put the lid on tightly and display your sand art in a prominent place.

Coin Bank

Scissors
Paper
Small can with plastic lid

Stickers and/or markers
Glue
Clear contact paper

Trim the paper so it completely covers the outside of the can. Have your child decorate the paper with stickers and/or markers.

Glue the decorated paper onto the can and cover it with clear contact paper. In the lid, cut a slit big enough for coins to pass through it and put the lid on the can.

Beaded Coaster

Glue
Large metal jar lid (or shallow plastic lid from small yogurt container)
Several same-size beads in a variety of colors
Magnetic strip (optional)

Spread glue on the inside of the lid. Help your child pour the beads onto the lid in a random design, or help him arrange them in a pattern. When the glue is dry, set a small plant on the coaster or use it to hold a drinking glass or mug. If you like, glue a magnetic strip onto the back of the coaster and display it on the refrigerator or other metal surface.

Easy Embroidery

Embroidery is the art of creating a design on cloth or other material with a needle and thread. This activity is an easy way for your child to learn or practice sewing skills.

*Markers and yarn in several
  matching colors*
Burlap
Pencil and paper (optional)

Scissors
Large-eye blunt needle
Casing (optional)

Let your child draw a picture or design on the burlap with the markers. He may want to sketch the design on paper first. Encourage him to keep the picture fairly simple. When his picture is complete, he can begin outlining the design with the yarn.

Cut the yarn into 2-foot lengths. Thread the needle with yarn in a color that matches the color of the outline. Tie the yarn behind the eye and at the end so it won't pull through. Show your child how to outline the picture he's drawn by pushing the needle through the burlap from the back, and then pushing it back through the fabric from the front and pulling the thread.

When the embroidery is complete, you might like to sew a casing at the top of the burlap so your child's art can be displayed.

Moss Wreath

White glue
Small container
Water
Paintbrush
Styrofoam form (heart-shaped or circular)
Spanish moss
Ribbon (in several colors, if desired)
Baby's breath or silk flowers (optional)

Pour the glue into the container and thin it with a little water. Brush the glue mixture onto the Styrofoam form, then have your child press Spanish moss onto the glue. If necessary, use additional glue and moss to fill in any empty spaces. When the glue is dry, wind ribbon around the wreath. Begin and end at the top of the wreath, tying the ends in a bow. If you like, use more than one color of ribbon, and tuck baby's breath or silk flowers into the moss.

Pinless Bulletin Board

Heavy cardboard
Gift-wrap, colored paper, or colored or patterned contact
  paper
Tape
Scissors
Rubber bands
Ribbon or yarn

Cover the cardboard with gift-wrap. Cut four to six equally spaced slits along each edge. Help your child stretch the rubber bands both horizontally and vertically across the board, inserting the bands in the slits, to make a grid. Poke two holes several inches apart along one edge. Thread ribbon through the holes and tie the ends together to form a loop for hanging.

Slide notes, photos, lists, and reminders under the rubber bands.

Painted Pot

This colorful pot can be used for more than just plants! Fill it with candies and give it as a gift or use it to hold earrings, spare change, or candles.

Terra cotta pot   *Sponges*
Acrylic paints   *Small stickers*
Paintbrushes   *Clear acrylic spray*

Have your child paint a terra cotta pot using one of the following techniques:

- Paint the outside of the pot one color. Paint the rim and inside a different color.
- Paint the pot one color inside and out. When the paint is dry, use sponges to dab on two or three other colors.
- Paint the pot one color inside and out. When the paint is dry, stick small stickers on the outside of the pot. Paint the outside of the pot again with a different color. Remove the stickers when the second coat of paint is dry.

When the paint is completely dry, spray your pot with clear acrylic spray.

Beautiful Butterfly

Coffee filter or paper towel
Paint and paintbrush, markers, or food coloring and eye-
  dropper
Clothespin
Scissors
Pipe cleaner
Glue
Magnet

Help your child color a coffee filter with paint, markers, or
food coloring diluted with water and applied with an eyedropper. When the coffee filter is dry, twist it in the center to
form a bow tie shape and clip a clothespin onto it. Cut the
pipe cleaner into small lengths for antennae. Glue on pipe
cleaner antennae. Glue a magnet onto the back and display
the butterfly on your refrigerator or other metal surface.

Clay Mosaic

Modeling Clay (See Appendix A.)
Rolling pin
Knife
Baking sheet
Fine sandpaper
Paintbrushes and paint in a variety of colors
Heavy cardboard or matte board
Glue gun or craft glue
Clear acrylic spray (optional)

Make a batch of Modeling Clay. Preheat your oven to 250°F. Help your child roll the clay on a lightly floured surface until it's about ⅛ inch thick. Cut the clay into 1-inch squares and place them on a baking sheet and bake for 30 minutes, then turn them over and bake for another 90 minutes. When the squares are cool, sand them, then paint them in a variety of colors.

When the paint is dry, have your child arrange the squares on the cardboard. Glue them into place. If you like, finish the mosaic with clear acrylic spray.

Candy Jar

Assorted wrapped candies　　　*Scissors*
Small canning or baby food　　*Fabric*
　jar with lid　　　　　　　　*Ribbon*

Allow your child to choose favorites from an assortment of wrapped candies. As he drops each candy in the jar, talk about its color, smell, shape, and so on. If you like, count the candies as they're dropped into the jar.

　　When your child has filled the jar to his satisfaction, put on the lid. Cut a circle from the fabric to cover the lid and tie it on with the ribbon. Label the jar however you like.

Potpourri Air Freshener

8-inch length of ribbon　　*Masking tape*
Metal jar lid or lid from　　*Craft glue*
　frozen juice can　　　　*Potpourri*

Attach the ends of the ribbon to the lid with masking tape. Cover the lid with craft glue, then help your child press potpourri into the glue until the lid is completely covered. Let the glue dry, then hang the air freshener in a closet, bathroom, vehicle, or anywhere you want to smell sweet.

Candle Art

Sheet of beeswax
Newspaper and wax paper
Ruler or straightedge
Utility knife

Scissors
Candlewick
Glitter and beeswax in
*   another color (optional)*

Place the beeswax on newspaper covered with wax paper. Use a ruler and a utility knife to cut the wax in half along the long edge so you have two rectangles, or in thirds along the short edge so you have three rectangles.

Place one of the wax rectangles in front of you so its short edge is near you. Cut a length of candlewick 2 inches longer than this edge. Lay the wick on the wax along this edge so an inch of wick sticks out beyond each end. Starting at this edge, help your child slowly roll up the wax and press it into the wick. Work slowly so the warmth of his hands softens the wax. Continue rolling the wax, trying to keep the perpendicular edge (which will be the bottom of the candle) even. When you've finished, press the edge of the wax firmly into the candle. Gently tap the bottom of the candle on your work surface to even it out. Trim the wick to ½ inch at the top of the candle and cut off the wick at the bottom.

If you like, roll the candle in glitter, or cut out a small shape from another color of beeswax and gently press it onto the candle.

Cup of Cocoa

Cocoa ingredients

6½ cups dry milk
1 package noninstant
  chocolate pudding mix
1 cup chocolate drink mix
½ cup powdered nondairy
  creamer
½ cup powdered sugar
½ cup unsweetened cocoa
  powder

Ziploc bags
Decorative mugs
Scissors
Cellophane
Ribbon
Index cards
Pen or marker

Have your child pour the cocoa ingredients into a large bowl
and mix well. Pour enough cocoa mix into Ziploc bags so the
bags can be sealed and placed into the decorative mugs.
Place each mug on a square of cellophane. Gather the cellophane corners at the top and wrap ribbon around them and
tie a tight knot. (Or pour the mix into a small coffee can that
your child has decorated. Or pour it into small canning jars.
Cut circles from fabric to cover the lids and tie them on with
ribbon.) Write the following instructions on each index card:
"Hot Cocoa Mix: Stir ⅓ cup cocoa mix into 1 cup boiling
water." Poke a hole in a corner of the card and thread a ribbon end through it, then tie it off.

Cappuccino Gift Mix

Cappuccino ingredients
⅔ cup instant coffee crystals
1 cup powdered nondairy creamer
1 cup chocolate drink mix
½ cup sugar
¾ teaspoon ground cinnamon
⅜ teaspoon ground nutmeg

Food processor or rolling pin
Small coffee can (with lid), wrapped with construction
   paper and decorated with markers or stickers
Index card
Pen or marker

Grind the coffee crystals in a food processor or crush them with a rolling pin. Combine the crystals with the rest of the cappuccino ingredients in a bowl. Let your child decorate the coffee can, then pour the cappuccino mix into the can. (Or pour the mix into small canning jars. Cut circles from fabric to cover the lids and tie them on with ribbon.) Write the following instructions on an index card: "Cappuccino Mix: Stir ¼ cup cappuccino mix into 1 cup boiling water." Attach the card to the can.

Spiced Tea Treat

Tea ingredients
½ cup instant tea powder
1 cup sweetened lemonade mix
1 cup orange-flavored drink mix
1 teaspoon ground cinnamon
½ teaspoon ground cloves

Small canning jars
Scissors
Fabric
Ribbon
Index cards
Pen or marker

Have your child combine the tea ingredients in a bowl and mix them well. Pour the tea mix into the jars. Cut circles from fabric to cover the lids and tie them on with ribbon. (Or pour the mix into Ziploc bags, then place the bags in decorative mugs and wrap with cellophane and ribbon.) Write the following instructions on each index card: "Spiced Tea Mix: Stir 3 teaspoons of tea mix into 1 cup boiling water." Poke a hole in a corner of each card and thread a ribbon end through it, then tie it off.

No-Sew Cape

This cape is so easy to make and is a fun addition to your dress-up box.

1 yard of felt
Straight pins
Scissors
Ribbon
Fabric paints, glitter, beads, sequins, or other decorative
trimmings

Fold up about 2 inches of felt along one of the long edges. Pin it into place. Cut slits about every 2 inches along this fold, being careful not to cut through to the edge. Remove the pins. Weave ribbon through the slits and gather the felt. If you like, tie each ribbon end around the end slits so it can't be pulled out. Have your child decorate the cape with fabric paints and other trimmings.

Fabric Batik

Batik is usually done with hot wax, but this flour-and-water method is safer and easier, and it creates beautiful batik designs.

4 tablespoons flour
3 tablespoons water
Bowl
Paintbrush
Cotton handkerchief or pillowcase
Cold-water dye
Knife

Mix the flour and water together in a bowl to make a smooth paste. Help your child paint a thick layer of paste all over the handkerchief. Let the paste dry completely (drying time may be several hours). When dry, scrunch the fabric so the paste cracks all over. Prepare the cold-water dye according to the package directions. Soak the handkerchief in the dye for about an hour. Rinse it thoroughly in cold water and allow it to dry. Scrape off any leftover paste with a knife, then rinse the handkerchief again. Wash it in soapy water and let it dry.

CD Picture Frame

Scissors
Colored or construction paper
Empty CD case
Photo of your child, friends, or family
Paint pens, glitter glue, beads, buttons, craft foam shapes,
*   and other decorative materials*
Glue gun
Pipe cleaner or craft wire

Cut a square from the colored paper so it fits into the front
of the CD case. Trim a photo as necessary and glue it onto
the paper. Insert the paper into the CD case. Have your child
decorate the case around the photo with paint pens and other
decorative materials. Use a glue gun to attach a pipe cleaner
loop to the back of the frame for hanging.

Necktie Snake

Old necktie
Straight pins
Needle and thread
Scissors
Red felt

Craft glue or glue gun
Googly eyes
Funnel
Rice

Fold down the open edges at the wide end of an old necktie so they're lined up. (You should have a pointed end that widens and then narrows down the length of the tie.) Pin then sew the edges together. This is the snake's head. Sew a narrow rectangle of red felt to the pointed end for the snake's tongue. About 2 inches from the pointed end, glue on two googly eyes. Holding the tie so the snake's head hangs down, have your child use a funnel to fill it with rice. Sew the narrow end of the tie shut.

If you like, make mother and baby snakes by first cutting the tie so the mother has about two-thirds of the length, the baby about one-third.

Easy Fabric Wreath

Using fabric in seasonal or holiday colors makes this a practical craft to make and give any time of the year.

Scissors or pinking shears
Fabric
12-inch Styrofoam wreath
Pencil
Other decorations (pine cones, holiday shapes cut from craft foam, a flag, or whatever suits the occasion)
Ribbon

Use scissors to cut the fabric into 2-inch squares. Show your child how to poke the center of each fabric square (wrong side down) into the Styrofoam wreath with the sharpened end of the pencil. Work around the wreath until it's completely covered with fabric. If you like, add other decorations. Choose ribbon in a complementary color, wrap it around the wreath, and tie it in a bow.

T-Shirt Art

Scissors
Contact paper
Prewashed cotton T-shirt
Newspaper
1 cup warm water
1 teaspoon salt
1 tablespoon Rit Liquid Dye
Bowl
Small plastic spray bottle
Sponge or absorbent cloth

Cut words, letters, numbers, or other shapes from the contact paper. Remove the backing and stick the contact paper
shapes onto the T-shirt. Place several layers of newspaper
inside the T-shirt to prevent the dye from soaking through.
Combine the water, salt, and liquid dye in a bowl and pour
the mixture into the spray bottle. Help your child spray the
T-shirt around the shapes. If you like, prepare another color
of dye and spray it on the shirt. Lightly dab the shapes with a
sponge to absorb the paint. Remove the shapes and let the
T-shirt dry before wearing it.

Party Favors

Scissors
Gift-wrap or tissue paper
Toilet paper or paper towel rolls
Rubber bands
Tape
Small wrapped candies, toys, or other treats
Ribbon

Cut a small square of gift-wrap to cover the end of the toilet paper roll. Secure it with a rubber band or tape. Stand the roll so the covered end is on the bottom and have your child fill it with treats. Cover the open end the same way as the first end.

Lay the roll on its side on gift-wrap that's 5 or 6 inches wider than the length of the roll, making sure there's an equal amount of gift-wrap sticking out beyond each end of the roll. Wrap the gift-wrap around the roll, and tape it in place. Tie ribbon around each end of the roll to make a party favor.

CHAPTER 11
Holiday Arts and Crafts

Slow down and enjoy life. It's not only the scenery you miss by going too fast—you also miss the sense of where you are going and why.

—Eddie Cantor

While it's true holidays and special celebrations can disrupt routines and be time consuming and expensive, they also provide necessary breaks from everyday life for both children and adults. Holiday celebrations are an important way to emphasize family traditions to your child, and they're a great way to use her artistic and creative abilities to make decorations, cards, gifts, gift-wrap, and more.

Start your preparations a week or two before each celebration, and allow your child to help you plan and prepare in whatever way she's able. Working together on seasonal arts and crafts is a fun way to anticipate the coming celebration, and for young children, anticipation is an important part of each holiday. As Anne Shirley says in Lucy Maud Montgomery's *Anne of Green Gables,* "[L]ooking forward to things is half the pleasure of them. You mayn't get the things themselves; but nothing can prevent you from having the fun of looking forward to them."

For each holiday, don't rely just on the projects I've included in this chapter. Use the drawing, painting, modeling, and other techniques found in previous chapters to create decorations, cards, and gift-wrap in seasonal colors. And if your child likes a particular project, say, Popcorn Pumpkins, modify it by using red Jell-O mix and shaping hearts for Valentine's Day or by using green Jell-O mix and making Christmas trees for Christmas.

Most toddlers are too young to understand the significance of each holiday, but include them in preparations whenever you can. Try to choose an open-ended project whenever possible—for example, finger painting in orange for Halloween or gluing green tissue paper scraps onto construction paper for Saint Patrick's Day. If you do choose an outcome-oriented project, remember to let your toddler do the things she's able to do. Help her when necessary, but try to focus on your toddler's participation, not the finished product.

VALENTINE'S DAY (FEBRUARY 14)

Valentine's Day is for celebrating love. Although no one is quite sure how Valentine's Day and its traditions started, most of us enjoy sharing cards, sweets, hugs, and kisses with those we love.

Valentine celebrations for young children can be kept simple. Read a book or two about Valentine's Day, like *It's Valentine's Day* by Jack Prelutsky (Mulberry Books, 1996), in the days leading up to February 14. Bake and ice some heart-shaped cookies to give to friends and neighbors. Use some of the drawing, painting, printmaking, or other techniques described in previous chapters to create Valentine's Day decorations, cards, and gifts. On Valentine's Day, dress the whole family in red and put your heart-shaped cookie cutter to work for toast, sandwiches, cheese, and finger Jell-O. A family dinner or small party with a few friends is a simple and fun way to celebrate this special day.

Stuffed Hearts

Large sheets of paper (each at least 2 square feet)
Tape or stapler
Markers, crayons, paint, and/or paintbrushes
Scissors
Newspaper, tissue paper, or other paper scraps
Hole punch and yarn (optional)

Lay a sheet of paper on top of another and tape or staple the edges together. Draw the outline of a heart on one side of the paper. Cut along the outline to make two cutouts. Tape or staple the edges of the cutouts together, leaving an opening along one edge.

   Let your child color or paint both sides of the heart red, white, and/or pink. Crumple up newspaper and stuff the heart with it. Staple the opening shut. If you like, punch a hole in the top of the shape. Loop yarn through the hole and hang the heart from a wall or ceiling.

Stencil Hearts

Pencil
Paper plate
Scissors
Red, white, or pink construction paper
Sponge
Red, white, and/or pink tempera paint
Clear contact paper (optional)
Marker (optional)

Draw a heart on the center of a paper plate. Cut out the heart by poking through the center of the heart and cutting from the inside out so the rim of the plate stays intact.

Hold the paper plate stencil against the construction paper. Have your child dip the sponge into the paint and dab it over the stencil. Lift the stencil, move it to another part of the paper, then dab again. Continue dabbing and moving the stencil until the paper is covered with hearts.

When the paint is dry, use the painting as a greeting card, or cover it with clear contact paper and use it as a Valentine's Day place mat. If you like, use a marker to write love messages on each heart.

Valentine Bookmarks

Scissors
Red or pink plus a contrasting color craft foam or felt
White glue

Cut heart shapes from the red or pink craft foam or felt. Cut 2-by-6-inch craft foam or felt strips in a contrasting color. Have your child glue the heart cutouts onto the strips to make Valentine's Day bookmarks.

Hidden Messages

White crayon or wax candle
White paper
Red or pink tempera paints
Paintbrush

Use a white crayon or wax candle to write a valentine message on the paper. Have your child paint over the paper to see the picture or message.

Valentine Place Cards

Heart-shaped cookie cutter
Pencil
Red or pink construction paper
Scissors
Markers, stickers, glitter glue, and so on
Glue or tape
Popsicle sticks
Baby food jars or small clay pots
Play dough
Candy on sticks like lollipops, suckers, and so on (optional)

Use the cookie cutter to trace heart shapes onto the paper.
Cut out the shapes and write a valentine's name on the center of each heart. Have your child decorate the hearts with
markers and so on. Glue or tape a Popsicle stick to the back
of each heart. Fill the jars or pots with play dough and insert
a heart into each. If you like, decorate the pots first (see page
271) and insert the candy on sticks.

Shortbread Valentine Cookies

2 cups butter
1 cup brown sugar
4¼ cups all-purpose flour
Heart-shaped cookie cutter
Colored sugar or other cookie decorations

Preheat your oven to 300°F. In a bowl, cream the butter and brown sugar. Mix in the flour thoroughly with your hands, a spoon, or an electric mixer. Place the dough on wax paper and roll it out until it's about ¼ inch thick. Help your child cut out shortbread hearts with the cookie cutter. Transfer the hearts to a baking sheet and sprinkle on colored sugar or other cookie decorations. Bake the hearts for about 15 minutes or until golden brown. The yield for this recipe will depend on the size of the cookie cutter you use.

Puffed Wheat Kisses

Scissors
Paper
Marker
Puffed Wheat Treats
  (See page 220.)

Funnel
Cooking spray
12-inch square of
  aluminum foil

Cut the paper into 8½-by-1-inch strips. Write or have your child write a Valentine's Day message on each strip. Make a batch of Puffed Wheat Treats and let the mixture cool slightly. Spray the inside of a funnel with cooking spray. Press the mixture into the funnel. Gently remove the cereal kiss and place it flat side down on the foil. Pull the corners of the foil up around the kiss. Insert a paper strip so half the strip sticks out the top of the kiss. Twist the foil ends at the top. This recipe makes 6–8 large kisses.

If you like, use Crispy Rice Treats (see page 204) instead of Puffed Wheat Treats to make
Crispy Rice Kisses.

SAINT PATRICK'S DAY (MARCH 17)

Saint Patrick's Day celebrates the patron saint of Ireland. Bishop Patrick introduced Christianity to Ireland during the fifth century, and in Ireland he's still honored with a national holiday and a week of religious festivities.

Regardless of your nationality or faith, celebrating Saint Patrick's Day can help break the monotony of the end of winter. For young children, preparations and celebrations need not be lavish nor complicated. Use some of the drawing, painting, printmaking, or other techniques described in previous chapters to create Saint Patrick's Day decorations. On Saint Patrick's Day, dress the family in green and invite a few friends over for a small party. Make a craft together and play a game or two. Decorate sugar cookies or cupcakes with green frosting and serve limeade or green Kool-Aid. If you like, listen to a recording of Irish folk music or read a book like *Jamie O'Rourke and the Big Potato* by Tomie dePaola (Paper Star, 1997).

Scented Shamrock

Scissors
Construction paper
Paintbrush
Glue
1 box green Jell-O mix
Empty saltshaker or spice container
Paintbrush
Hole punch and ribbon or string (optional)

Cut a shamrock shape from the construction paper. Have
your child paint glue all over the cutout. Pour the Jell-O mix
into the shaker and sprinkle the powder on the glue. Shake
off any excess powder and let the glue dry. Use the shamrock
as a greeting card, or punch a hole in its top, loop ribbon or
string through the hole, and hang it from a doorknob or picture hook.

Shamrock Magnet

Scissors
Cardboard
White glue
Small container
Green food coloring
Paintbrush
Dry spaghetti
Scissors
Magnet

Cut a shamrock shape from the cardboard. Pour a small amount of glue into the container. Add a few drops of green food coloring and mix well. Have your child paint the green glue all over the shamrock shape. Break the spaghetti into pieces about as wide as the shamrock. Cover the entire shamrock with rows of spaghetti. (The pieces can extend past the edges.) Brush green glue on the spaghetti and let it dry. Carefully trim the spaghetti. Glue a magnet onto the back of the shamrock.

Paddy's Day Paint

1 package instant vanilla pudding mix or whipping cream
2 small containers
Blue food coloring
Yellow food coloring
Baby food jar with lid and ¼ cup milk (optional)

Prepare the pudding according to package directions, or use whipping cream instead. Divide the pudding into the containers. Add a few drops of blue food coloring to one container and a few drops of yellow to the other. Let your child finger paint with the colored pudding on a tabletop or tray.

If you like, place 2 tablespoons of the instant pudding mix in a baby food jar with the milk and 3 drops each of blue and yellow food coloring. Close the lid tightly and have your child shake the jar until the pudding thickens.

Green Collage

Pen or marker
Construction paper
Green tissue paper and/or crepe paper
Magazines and catalogs (optional)
Glue

Trace the outline of a large shamrock on the construction paper. Have your child tear the tissue paper into small pieces or look through old magazines and catalogs and tear out any green pictures. Glue the green paper onto the construction paper to fill in the shamrock.

Shamrock Prints

Green paint   *Cardboard*
Shallow container   *Empty thread spool*
Paper   *Glue*
Knife   *Tape*
Green pepper   *3 small cans or baby food*
Scissors   *jars*

Use one of the following techniques to make shamrock prints for cards or other Saint Patrick's Day decorations:

- Pour the paint into the container. Dip your child's palm and four fingers in the paint (don't paint the thumb). Press her hand onto paper, dip it in the paint again, and press it again two times in a circular pattern, fingers pointing to the center, to make a shamrock shape.
- Cut a green pepper in half horizontally. Have your child grasp the top half by the stem, press it in the paint, then press it onto paper.
- Cut a heart shape from cardboard and glue it onto the empty thread spool. Have your child dip the shape in paint, then press it onto paper. Make two more heart prints, placing them so the pointed tips touch, to make a shamrock shape.
- Tape the small cans together in a circle. Have your child press the bottoms of the cans into the paint then onto paper.

Punch-Out Shamrock

Pencil
Green construction paper
Piece of Styrofoam or thin carpet
Large pushpin
Hole punch (optional)

Draw the outline of a shamrock on the paper. Place the paper on top of the Styrofoam or carpet piece. Have your child use a pushpin to punch holes in the paper along the outline. Hang the paper in front of a window to see the light shine through the holes.

If you like, draw a shamrock outline on a half-sheet of green construction paper. Use a hole punch to punch holes along the outline, then hang the shamrock.

Irish Toast

2 tablespoons milk
Green food coloring
Small container
New paintbrush
White bread
Toaster
Butter

Mix the milk with a few drops of green food coloring in the
container. Help your child paint shamrocks or other designs
on the bread. Toast the bread and butter it. Eat it as it is, or
use the toast to make a Saint Patrick's Day sandwich.

EASTER (DATE VARIES)

Easter is a Christian holiday that celebrates the resurrection of Jesus Christ. It's also a time to celebrate the coming of spring and all its delightful signs of new life.

This holiday can help bring sunshine to the last few days of winter, so begin your Easter preparations a week or two in advance. Use some of the drawing, painting, printmaking, or other techniques described in previous chapters to create Easter decorations, cards, and gifts. Have an informal parade in your neighborhood with decorated bicycles, wagons, and tricycles. Decorate eggs or make candy together. Host a family dinner or small get-together with friends where kids can make a simple craft and play a few games. Hold an egg or candy hunt outdoors or in, depending on the weather.

Easy Egg Mosaic

Crayon, pen, or marker
Construction paper
Glue
Colored eggshells (See page 306 to make your own.)
Scissors
Clear contact paper
Tape
Tissue paper in pastel colors

Use one of the following methods to create a beautiful egg mosaic:

- Have your child draw an egg shape on construction paper. Fill in the shape with glue and press on small pieces of colored eggshells.
- Cut an egg shape from clear contact paper. Tape the contact paper sticky side up to a table or other flat surface, and have your child press colored eggshells onto the egg.
- Tear the tissue paper into small pieces. Cut an egg shape from clear contact paper. Tape the contact paper sticky side up to a table or other flat surface, and have your child press the paper pieces onto the egg.

Egg Decorating

For the following activities, use hard-boiled eggs. Set them on an upside down egg carton to dry. Store them in the refrigerator if you plan to eat them.

- Pour ½ cup of water into each of several saucepans (one for each color). Have your child add a different cut-up fruit, vegetable, or plant to each pan. (Try carrots, grass, blueberries, and coffee grounds.) Bring the water to a boil and simmer it until it turns the color you want. Strain and reserve the water. When it cools, soak the eggs in it.
- Have your child soak crepe paper in hot water in small containers (one for each color). Soak the eggs in the water.
- Measure ¼ teaspoon of food coloring into each of several small bowls (one for each color). Add ¾ cup of hot water and 1 tablespoon of white vinegar. Soak the eggs in the water.
- Grate crayon stubs. Fill a big glass jar with very hot water. Drop pinches of grated crayon in the water. When the crayon begins to melt, add an egg. Have your child twirl the egg in the water with a slotted spoon. The wax will make a design on the egg. Carefully remove the egg with the spoon.

Egg Roll Art

Paper
Shallow box or baking pan
Tempera paint in Easter colors
Hard-boiled eggs
Clear contact paper (optional)

Place paper in the bottom of the box. Pour a small amount of paint on the paper, then place 1 or 2 hard-boiled eggs in the box. Have your child tilt and rotate the box to move the eggs around and through the paint. If you like, add another color of paint and repeat the process. Let the paper dry then hang it to display, or cover it with clear contact paper to make an Easter place mat.

Hot Cross Buns

⅓ cup lukewarm water
2 teaspoons sugar
2 tablespoons active dry
   yeast
⅓ cup milk
½ cup butter or margarine
¼ cup sugar
1 teaspoon salt
4 cups flour

1 teaspoon ground
   cinnamon
3 eggs, beaten
⅔ cup currants
1 egg white
1 tablespoon cold water
Powdered sugar
Water

Pour the lukewarm water into a small bowl. Add 2 teaspoons
sugar and stir to dissolve it. Sprinkle the yeast over the water
and let it stand for 10 minutes, then have your child stir it well.

In a saucepan heat the milk and butter to scalding.
Remove the pan from the heat and pour the scalded mixture
into a large bowl. Add ¼ cup sugar and the salt. Sift 1 cup
flour with the cinnamon and add it to the milk mixture, stirring it to blend. Add the eggs and beat the mixture until it's
smooth. Stir in the yeast mixture and the currants.

Add enough of the remaining flour to make a soft dough.
Have your child mix it thoroughly with her hands, then turn
it out onto a lightly floured surface and knead it until it's
smooth.

Place the dough in a large greased bowl, cover it with a
damp cloth, and let it rise in a warm place until it's doubled

(about 1½ hours). Punch the dough down and let it rise again for a half-hour. Have your child shape the dough into 16 round buns and place them in a greased 13-by-9-inch pan. Use a sharp knife to cut a cross in the top of each bun. Let the buns rise for about 1 hour.

Preheat your oven to 375°F. Beat the egg white and cold water together and brush the mixture over the buns. Bake them for about 15 minutes or until they're well browned and baked through.

Mix a little powdered sugar and water to make a thick glaze, and let your child spoon it into the crosses on top of the buns while they're still slightly warm.

Bird's Nest Snack

¼ cup butter
4 cups miniature marshmallows or 40 large marshmallows
5 cups crispy rice cereal (pastel-colored, if available)
Candy eggs or other Easter candy
⅓ cup chocolate or butterscotch chips (optional)
1 cup chow mein noodles (optional)

Melt the butter in a large saucepan. Add the marshmallows and stir the mixture constantly over low heat until it's syrupy. Turn off the heat. Stir in the cereal until it's well coated. Have your child form some of the mixture into a nest shape with her hands. Repeat this process with the remaining mixture. Place a few candy eggs in each nest.

If you like, melt the chocolate or butterscotch chips and mix them with the chow mein noodles, then use this mixture instead to form nest shapes.

Fuzzy Chick Picture

Pencil or pen
Paper
Crayons or markers
Glue
Googly eyes (optional)
Scissors
Yellow yarn
Heavy paper or cardboard (optional)
Popsicle stick (optional)

Draw the outline of a chick on the paper. Have your child color in the chick's feet, beak, and eyes. Glue on googly eyes if you like. Snip the yarn into tiny pieces to make yellow fuzz. Spread glue on the parts of your chick you want fuzzy. Sprinkle the yellow fuzz on the chick and press it lightly with your finger to make it stick.

If you'd like to make a fuzzy chick stick puppet, glue your picture onto heavy paper, cut out the chick, and glue it onto a Popsicle stick.

Eggs in the Grass

Glue
Construction paper
Plastic grass
Baby food jar lid or other small container
White or colored cotton balls

Spread the glue on the paper. Have your child press plastic grass on the glue. Pour a little glue into a baby food jar lid. Dip the cotton balls in glue and nestle them in the grass.

CANADA DAY (JULY 1)

Canada Day is Canada's birthday. It honors the anniversary of Canada's confederation in 1867. The celebration of Canada Day differs from family to family, but it usually includes a parade, a picnic or barbecue with family and friends, and fireworks at night.

Help your child understand why Canada celebrates this day and do a few simple things to begin building Canada Day traditions with your family. Your family's traditions will help your child feel proud of her country. (Even if you're not Canadian, your child is sure to enjoy learning about Canada and doing the activities on the following pages.) Use some of the drawing, painting, printmaking, or other techniques described in previous chapters to create red and white decorations and cards. Wear red and white clothes, fly the Canadian flag, and sing Canadian folksongs. Bake a birthday cake, light a few candles, and sing "Happy Birthday" to Canada.

Flag Fun

One sheet each red and white construction paper (same size)
Scissors
Pencil and maple leaf

Glue
Tape and dowel
Clear contact paper
White poster board
Red paint, marker, or crayon

- Fold the red paper into thirds along the long side, then unfold it. Cut along both folds to make three equal strips of red paper. Draw or trace a maple leaf onto one of the strips and cut it out. Lay the white paper on the table with a long side facing you. Have your child glue one red strip onto the left side of the white paper and the other red strip onto the right side. Glue the maple leaf onto the middle of the white strip. Tape the flag to a dowel and wave it proudly.
- Follow the above directions, but rather than taping the flag to a dowel, cover it with clear contact paper to make a place mat.
- Make a flag poster by marking off white poster board into thirds. Have your child paint or color each outside third red, then paint or color a red maple leaf in the center third.

Maple Leaf Place Mats

Scissors
Sponge
Red liquid tempera paint

White construction paper
Clear contact paper

Cut the sponge into a maple leaf shape. Have your child dip
it into the paint, then press it onto the construction paper.
When the paint is dry, cover the paper with clear contact
paper and use it as a place mat at a Canada Day picnic.

Red-and-White Painting

You may want to donate the salad spinner to the craft box
after you do this activity.

Old salad spinner
Black or dark-colored
  construction paper

Scissors
Red and white paint

Remove the insert from the spinner. Cut a circle from the
paper so it fits into the bottom of the spinner (trace around
the bottom of the insert if you like). Replace the insert on top
of the paper. Dribble a little red paint into the spinner, then
put the lid on and have your child spin the spinner. Repeat
this process with the white paint, then remove the paper from
the spinner and let the painting dry.

Fireworks Painting

*Koosh ball or plastic
   scouring pad
Liquid tempera paint*

*Dark-colored construction
   paper
Glue
Glitter*

Have your child dip the ball or pad into the paint, then press it onto the paper. Change colors and press it again. Let the paint dry. Dip the ball or pad into glue and press it onto the paper, then sprinkle it with glitter.

Maple Leaf Snacks

*White frosting or cream cheese
2 small containers
Red food coloring
Maple-leaf-shaped cookies or graham crackers
Small plastic knife or Popsicle stick*

Divide the frosting equally into the containers. Add a few drops of the food coloring to one container and mix it well. If you like, add more food coloring. Have your child spread the white and red frosting onto the cookies.

Picnic Collage

Red marker or tempera paint and paintbrush
White construction paper
Small paper plate
Old magazines
Scissors
Glue
Black plastic ants or black marker (optional)

Draw or paint red horizontal and vertical lines on the paper to make a checked tablecloth design. Glue the paper plate onto the tablecloth. Help your child hunt through old magazines for pictures of food you'd like to eat at a holiday picnic. Cut out the pictures and glue them onto the plate. If you like, glue plastic ants (or draw them on with a marker) onto the tablecloth.

INDEPEDENCE DAY (JULY 4)

Independence Day celebrates the United States' adoption of the Declaration of Independence in 1776. This holiday is America's birthday. The celebration of Independence Day differs from family to family, but it usually includes a parade, a picnic or barbecue with family and friends, and fireworks at night.

While very young children will not easily grasp the concept of a nation's birthday, you can do a few simple things to begin building Independence Day traditions with your family. Your family traditions will help your child feel proud of her country. (Even if you're not American, your child is sure to enjoy learning about the United States and doing the crafts and making the treats on the following pages.) Use some of the drawing, painting, printmaking, or other techniques described in previous chapters to create red, white, and blue decorations and cards. Fly the U.S. flag, sing American folksongs, and dress in red, white, and blue. Bake a birthday cake, light a few candles, and sing "Happy Birthday" to the United States.

Fourth of July Noisemakers

*Small hard items (rocks, dry
  beans, popcorn kernels,
  pennies, and so on)
Frozen juice cans with lids*

*Tape
Red, white, and blue tissue
  paper
Twist-ties*

Place a few hard items inside each can. Tape on the lids. Roll
the cans in red, white, and blue tissue paper so there are several inches of tissue paper sticking out beyond each end of
the cans. Have your child twist the tissue paper together at
each end and secure with a twist-tie. Use the noisemakers in
a Fourth of July parade!

Old Glory Tablecloth

2 spray bottles
Water
Red and blue food coloring
White cotton sheet or tablecloth
Red and blue fabric paint (optional)

Partially fill the spray bottles with water. Add red food coloring to one bottle and blue to the other. Add enough coloring to get vivid shades of red and blue. Hang the sheet or tablecloth on a fence or lay it flat on the ground. Have your child spray-paint the sheet with the colored water. Let the sheet dry, then use it for a holiday tablecloth. (Diluted food coloring will easily wash out of most fabrics. For permanent color, use diluted fabric paint.)

Ice Cream Paint

Shaving cream
Glue
Bowl
Food coloring (optional)
Construction paper
Paintbrush, spoon, or Popsicle stick
Scissors
Colored candy sprinkles (optional)

Mix together equal parts of shaving cream and glue in a
bowl. Tint the mixture with food coloring if you like. Have
your child spread it on the paper with a paintbrush, spoon,
or Popsicle stick, or use it as finger paint. If you like, cut a
cone shape from construction paper and stick it into a mound
of paint to look like an upside down ice cream cone. Sprinkle
colored candy sprinkles on your melted ice cream picture.

Red, White, and Blue Cake

1 package white cake mix
One 3-ounce package vanilla
pudding mix
4 eggs
¼ cup vegetable oil

1 cup cold water
Red and blue food coloring
Frosting, sprinkles, paper
flags, or other decorations

Preheat your oven to 350°F. Grease a 9-by-13-inch pan. Beat the mixes, eggs, oil, and water until smooth. Divide the batter into 2 equal portions. Pour half the batter into the pan. Divide the remaining half into 2 equal portions. Color 1 portion with a few drops of red food coloring and the other with a few drops of blue. Have your child drop spoonfuls of colored batter onto the batter in the pan. Use a knife to swirl the colored batter into the white. Bake the cake 45–50 minutes. Let it cool, then frost and decorate it with sprinkles, paper flags, or whatever you like.

Cookie Hamburgers

White frosting
Red, yellow, and green food coloring
Empty plastic ketchup and mustard bottles
Shredded coconut
Round vanilla and chocolate wafer cookies

Tint a small amount of the frosting with red food coloring and spoon it into the ketchup bottle. Tint more frosting yellow and fill the mustard bottle with it. Use a few drops of green food coloring to tint the coconut.

For each "hamburger," you'll need two vanilla cookies and one chocolate one. Have your child squeeze some ketchup- or mustard-colored frosting onto one vanilla wafer. Place a chocolate "hamburger patty" on top. Add more frosting and some green coconut "lettuce." Top with more frosting and a second vanilla cookie. Eat the cookie burgers or refrigerate them for several hours and serve them as an Independence Day snack or dessert.

Fourth of July Window Hanging

Paintbrush
Glue thinned with water
Clear plastic plate
Red, white, and blue paper products (streamers, tissue paper, napkins, and so on)
Confetti stars and glitter (optional)
Poster putty

Brush the glue all over the plate. Have your child tear the paper products into small pieces and stick them onto the plate. Add confetti stars and glitter, if you like. Brush glue over the paper and glitter and allow the hanging to dry. Attach it to a window with poster putty.

HALLOWEEN (OCTOBER 31)

Halloween began in ancient times, and there is great debate over the origins of various aspects of the celebration. One thing is certain, however: People in Europe and North America have celebrated Halloween for many centuries.

Many of the stories, imagery, and/or customs surrounding Halloween can be particularly frightening to young children, so it's wise to be careful how you celebrate the holiday. You can, however, still enjoy Halloween by focusing on its seasonal aspects. Many churches and community centers host fall carnivals or Halloween parties where children can play games, eat food, and have fun together while avoiding the dangers associated with trick-or-treating. If you want to have a small Halloween party yourself, encourage guests to dress in fun (not frightening) costumes. Use some of the drawing, painting, printmaking, or other techniques described in previous chapters to make crafts in Halloween colors. Play a few games together, then decorate and eat some Halloween cookies, cupcakes, or other treats.

Lollipop Treats

Pipe cleaners
Large wrapped lollipops
Glue
Googly eyes
Scissors (optional)

Tissue
Rubber bands
Marker (optional)
Thread or string

Make the following Halloween lollipop treats:

- **Spiders:** Have your child twist four pipe cleaners around each lollipop stick. Bend and shape them to form spider legs. Glue two googly eyes onto the candy. (If you like, trim the stick just beyond the pipe cleaners.)
- **Ghosts:** Have your child cover each lollipop with a tissue. Wrap a rubber band just below the candy to form a ghost. If you like, use a marker to add a face. Attach thread or string to the ghosts and hang them from the ceiling or doorway.

Black Cat

Scissors
Construction paper, poster
 board, or pencil and paper
Black tissue paper
Paintbrush
Glue

Googly eyes
Toothpicks
Pink construction paper, craft
 foam, or yarn (optional)
Black yarn (optional)

Cut a simple cat shape from construction paper or draw the outline of a cat on paper. Tear or cut the tissue paper into small pieces. Have your child brush glue all over the cat, then press on the tissue paper pieces. Glue on googly eyes and toothpick whiskers. If you like, glue on a nose cut from pink construction paper, or fashioned from yarn.

If you like, use black yarn instead of tissue paper. Snip the yarn into tiny pieces to make fuzz. Sprinkle the fuzz on the cat and press it lightly with your finger to make it stick.

Beastly Bats

Black tempera or acrylic paint
Paintbrush
Clothespin (not one with a spring)
Black construction paper
Pencil or marker
Scissors
Glue
Red tempera or acrylic paint (optional)
String

Paint the clothespin and allow it to dry. Fold the paper in half so the short edges meet and draw the outline of a bat wing, starting and ending the outline at the fold. Cut out the wings, but don't cut the fold. Unfold the wings, squeeze glue along the outside fold, then press the wings onto the clothespin. If you like, add two dots of red paint to the clothespin for eyes. Tie a string to the bat and hang it from the ceiling.

Pumpkin Drawing

Small pumpkin
Washable markers
Damp paper towel

Allow your child to draw on the pumpkin with washable markers. The marker will wipe off with a damp paper towel so she can draw, wipe, and draw on her pumpkin again.

Chocolate Spiders

⅔ cup chocolate chips
Saucepan or microwave-safe bowl
2 cups chow mein noodles
Baking sheet
Wax paper
Small red candies

Melt the chocolate chips in a saucepan on the stove or melt them in a bowl in the microwave. Toss the noodles with the melted chocolate. Have your child drop spoonfuls of the mixture onto a baking sheet lined with wax paper. Add two candy eyes to each spider. Let the chocolate harden. Store the spiders in the refrigerator.

Spider Web

Black tempera paint
White or red paper plate
Black marker
Scissors
Tape

Black yarn
Plastic insects (optional)
Black paper plate, white
    tempera paint, and
    white yarn (optional)

Have your child dip her thumb into the black paint and press it onto the center of the plate. This will be the spider's body. When the paint is dry, draw on 8 spider legs.

Cut ½-inch slits at 1-inch intervals around the edge of the plate. Tape 1 end of the yarn to the back of the plate. Show your child how to wrap the yarn across the front and back of the plate, inserting it into the slits, to make a web. Make sure the web doesn't cover the spider. When the web is finished, trim any excess yarn and tape the end to the back of the plate. If you like, glue plastic insects onto the web.

If you like, use a black paper plate, or paint a white plate black. Use white paint and white yarn to make the spider and its web.

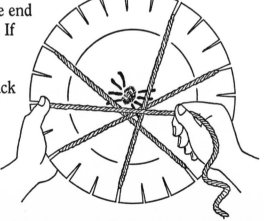

Pumpkin Math

Pumpkinseeds
11 paper plates
Marker
Glue
Scissors
Construction paper (orange and other colors)
Crayons or markers

- As you carve your Halloween pumpkin, save and dry the seeds. Ask your child to place the seeds in groups of twos, threes, fours, and so on. Ask your child to work out simple math problems with the seeds. For example, you could say, "I have five seeds. If I take two away, how many will I have left?"

- On each paper plate, have your child write one of the numbers from 0 to 10. Have her glue the appropriate number of pumpkinseeds onto each plate.

- Cut various sizes of pumpkin shapes from orange construction paper, cutting at least two shapes of each size. Let your child decorate the shapes with crayons or markers, or with eye, nose, and mouth shapes cut from construction paper. Give your child one pumpkin of each size and have her arrange the shapes from smallest to largest and largest to smallest. Give her all the shapes and have her match the pumpkins by size.

THANKSGIVING (DATE VARIES)

The first Thanksgiving celebration was held by the Pilgrims after their first harvest in 1621. Although many of the original settlers died that first year, the remaining Pilgrims were grateful for the abundance of their harvest and invited their Native American neighbors to join in their three-day feast.

Young children may not understand the significance of the holiday, but the sheer abundance of food on the table at most Thanksgiving celebrations makes this an excellent time to encourage a spirit of thankfulness in your child. Talk with your child about things for which you both are thankful. Use some of the drawing, painting, printmaking, or other techniques described in previous chapters to create Thanksgiving decorations and cards. Read a book like *The Thanksgiving Story* by Alice Dalgliesh (Aladdin Library, 1985).

You can also use Thanksgiving to encourage a giving spirit in your child and make a positive impact on your community. Donate canned food to a food bank. Set aside good, usable clothing and toys and take them to a local relief agency. Bake a plate of cookies or other treats for community workers or homebound friends. Invite someone who is alone to share your Thanksgiving celebration. Your child will learn just how good it can feel to share her blessings with others!

Autumn Colors Collage

White glue
Water
Liquid dish soap
Wax paper
Paintbrush
Scissors

Dark-colored construction
*   paper (optional)*
Contact paper, hole punch,
*   and ribbon (optional)*
Tissue paper scraps in fall
*   colors*

Thin the glue with water and a few drops of dish soap. Tear off a sheet of wax paper that's about twice as long as the collage you wish to create. Fold it in half, then open it.

Have your child brush the glue on one half of the wax paper, then stick the tissue paper scraps onto the glue. Brush more glue on top of the tissue paper, then fold the other half of the wax paper onto the design. Press and smooth the paper, then let it dry for several hours.

If you like, cut dark-colored paper strips and glue them around the edges of the collage as a frame. Or use one of these suggestions:

- Substitute clear contact paper (sticky side up) for wax paper and glue.
- Cut the finished collage into strips and use them as bookmarks. Punch a hole in the top of each bookmark and add a ribbon tassel.

Burlap Prints

Newsprint or construction paper
Tape
Burlap
Paintbrushes or sponges
Liquid tempera paint in fall colors (red, orange, yellow, brown)
Ribbon or yarn (optional)
Clear contact paper (optional)

Place the newsprint on a table or other work surface. Tape the burlap on the newsprint. Have your child use paintbrushes or sponges to paint the burlap in fall colors. When she's done, lift the burlap from the paper and allow both the burlap and the newsprint to dry. If you like, attach a loop of ribbon or yarn to the burlap and hang it to display. You can also cover the newsprint with clear contact paper to make a place mat, if you wish.

Spice Turkey

White glue
Shallow container
Construction paper, small paper plate, or small aluminum
  pie pan
Pumpkin pie spice, allspice, ground cinnamon, or ground
  nutmeg
Black and red markers

Pour the glue into the container. Dip your child's hand in the
glue and press it, fingers spread, onto the paper, plate, or pie
pan to make a handprint turkey. Have her sprinkle spices
onto the turkey. When the glue is
dry, use the black marker to
draw an eye and beak on
the thumb, and turkey
feet at the bottom of the
print. Use a red marker
to draw a wattle around
the beak.

Pumpkin Finger Paint

½ cup pumpkin pie filling
½ cup marshmallow creme
¼ cup whipped cream
  (or use frozen whipped
  topping, thawed)

Small bowl
Finger paint paper

Have your child combine the first 3 ingredients in the bowl to make pumpkin pudding. Let her use it to finger paint on the paper, highchair tray, or tabletop, or simply eat it.

Popcorn Pumpkins

¼ cup margarine
10½-ounce bag miniature marshmallows
Orange jelly powder, 4-serving size
12 cups popped popcorn
Licorice, candy corn, or other treats

Melt the margarine in a large saucepan. Add the marshmallows and stir until they're melted. Remove the pan from the heat and stir in the jelly powder. Add the popcorn and mix it well. Grease your child's hands, then let her form the popcorn mixture into pumpkins. If you like, decorate them with licorice, candy corns, or other treats.

Thanksgiving Thankfulness

Old magazines and family photos
Scissors
Glue
Construction paper
Clear contact paper
Index cards

Small box or empty coffee can
Brown poster board and leaf-colored (green, red, yellow, orange, and brown) construction paper

Give your child the magazines and photos and have her cut out pictures of things for which she is thankful. Use the pictures in one or more of the following ways:

- Glue the pictures onto construction paper and cover with clear contact paper for a Thanksgiving place mat.
- Glue the pictures onto index cards and place them inside a small box or empty coffee can. Each day, have your child choose one card. Talk about what is on the card and why she is thankful for it.
- Draw a tree trunk and branches on brown poster board. Cut leaf shapes from leaf-colored construction paper. Glue the pictures onto the leaves, then glue the leaves onto the branches. Display the tree as a reminder of your blessings.

Cornucopia Place Cards

Index cards or construction paper cut into 3-by-5-inch rec-
tangles
Scissors
Glue
Bugles snacks
Trix cereal
Marker
Magnet (optional)

Fold the index cards in half so the short edges meet and the
lines are on the inside. Lay the card flat. Have your child
glue a Bugle onto one half of each card, then glue Trix cereal
into the Bugle to make a cornucopia. Write a guest's name
on each place card.

If you like, glue Trix cereal into a Bugle. Glue a magnet
onto the back of the cornucopia and decorate your refrigerator for Thanksgiving.

HANUKKAH (DATES VARY)

Hanukkah, the most joyous and festive of Jewish holidays, lasts eight days and takes place in December—sometimes early and sometimes late in the month.

The Hebrew word *hanukkah* means "dedication." Hanukkah was first celebrated more than two thousand years ago. It commemorates a time when the temple in Jerusalem had been restored and was about to be rededicated. Only one day's supply of oil for the holy lamps was found, but the lamps miraculously burned for eight days! This is why Hanukkah is also called the Festival of Lights and why the main focus of the celebration is the lighting of candles. A menorah, a special nine-branch candleholder, is used each day throughout the celebration.

Every year, families gather to light the Hanukkah menorah, remember their ancestors' historic struggle for religious freedom, recite prayers of thanks, exchange gifts, eat special foods, play games, and retell the story of Hanukkah.

Even if your family isn't Jewish, celebrating Hanukkah in a simple way can be fun for young children. Use some of the drawing, painting, printmaking, or other techniques described in previous chapters to create blue, yellow, and white decorations and cards. Read a book about Hanukkah like *The Eight Nights of Hanukkah* by Judy Nayer (Troll Communications, 1998). Place a menorah in your window, eat potato latkes, play dreidel games, and have fun!

Hanukkah Shapes

Blue, yellow, or white construction paper
Scissors
Glue stick
Small shoebox with lid
Glitter
2 large rubber bands
Confetti, Colorful Creative Salt (see Appendix A), spices,
  jelly powder, drink mix, or crushed Froot Loops cereal
  (optional)

Cut some or all of the following Hanukkah shapes from the
paper: candle, elephant, hammer, Star of David, and so on.
Rub glue on one or both sides of the shapes. Put one shape
into the shoebox and pour in the glitter. Place the lid on the
shoebox and wrap the rubber bands around the box and lid.
Have your child shake the box to cover the shape with glitter.
Remove the shape from the box and allow the glue to dry.
Repeat this process for the other shapes.

　　If you like, use other colorful material instead of glitter.

Star of David

Marker
Paper
Wax paper
Stapler
Glue
Glitter

String
Blue or yellow construction
paper (optional)
Paintbrush and hole punch
(optional)

Draw the outline of a Star of David on the paper. Lay wax paper waxy side up on the outline and staple the edges of the wax paper to the paper. Have your child squeeze glue on the outline to make a Star of David shape on the wax paper. Sprinkle glitter over the glue and let it dry. When the glue is completely dry, peel the shape from the wax paper. Loop string through one point of the star and hang it to display.

If you like, cut two equilateral triangles from blue or yellow construction paper. Place one triangle upside down on the other and glue them together. Brush glue on the star and sprinkle glitter over it. Punch a hole in one point of the star. Loop string through the hole and hang the star to display.

Dreidel

A dreidel is a small spinning top used to play Hanukkah games. Follow these directions to make your own dreidel.

Single-serving milk or
  juice carton
Tape
Plain paper

Pen or marker
Scissors
¼-inch dowel or
  unsharpened pencil

Flatten the top of the carton and tape it down securely. Cover the carton with the paper. On each side, write one of the letters *N, G, H,* and *S* or the following Hebrew characters:

Shin Hay Gimel Noon

ש ה ג נ

These characters are the first letters in the four words of the Hebrew message *nes gadol hayah sham,* which means "A great miracle happened there." (Hebrew characters are read from right to left.)

   Poke a small hole in the centers of the top and bottom of the carton and push the dowel or pencil through both holes to make a spinning top.
Use the dreidel to play the following games:

- Use pennies, dry beans, raisins, candies, or other small items as tokens. Distribute the tokens evenly among the players. Each player puts one token into the center, making a pile called the pot. The players take turns spinning the dreidel. The letter that lands faceup determines what the player does:

  נ *N:* The player does nothing.

  ג *G:* The player takes the pot, and everyone puts in one more token before the next player spins.

  ה *H:* The player takes half the pot.

  שׁ *S:* The player puts one token in the pot.

  Whenever the pot is empty or contains only one token, every player puts in one token before the next player spins. The game is over when one player has won all the tokens and everyone else has nothing.

- Hebrew characters also have number values. נ is fifty, ג is three, ה is five, and שׁ is three hundred. When a player spins the dreidel, she wins the number of points corresponding to the Hebrew letter that lands faceup.

- If you like, make up your own dreidel games. For example, שׁ might mean the player must sing a song, נ might mean the player must jump up and down five times, and so on.

Hanukkah Cookies

Sugar cookie, gingerbread, or other rolled cookie dough
Paper and pencil
Scissors
Rolling pin
Plastic knife
White frosting
2 small Ziploc bags
Blue and yellow food coloring

Make a batch of rolled cookie dough. Chill the dough. While the dough chills, draw some traditional Hanukkah shapes on paper, including a candle, elephant, hammer, Star of David, and so on. Cut out the shapes. Roll out the cookie dough. Place the shapes on the dough and have your child use a plastic knife to cut around each shape (or simply use Hanukkah cookie cutters if available). Bake the shapes according to the recipe's directions.

When the cookies are cool, place a small amount of white frosting in each Ziploc bag. Add a drop or two of yellow food coloring to one bag and a drop or two of blue food coloring to the other. Seal the bags and let your child squish the bags to color the frosting. Cut a small corner off each bag and let your child decorate the cookies by squeezing the frosting onto the cookies.

Hanukkah Mosaic

White, blue, and/or yellow dot stickers
White, blue, and/or yellow construction paper

Give your child a supply of stickers and paper in a contrasting color. (For example, give her white and yellow stickers and blue paper.) Encourage her to make a picture, design, or pattern with the dots. Display the finished product or use it as a Hanukkah greeting card.

Menorah

A menorah consists of nine candles, one for each day of Hanukkah and one, called the shammes, to light the other candles.

10 empty thread spools
Strip of heavy cardboard
Glue
Aluminum foil (optional)
9 birthday candles
Play dough
10 large marshmallows
Ornamental Frosting
  (See Appendix A.)

Pretzel sticks
Shoebox
Sand
Paper and crayons or
  markers (optional)
Drill and tree branch or
  piece of driftwood

Help your child make a menorah in one or more of the following ways:

- Set 9 thread spools in a row on the cardboard and glue them into place. Glue the last spool on top of the center one for the shammes. (If you like, cover the outsides of the spools with aluminum foil first.) Insert the candles into the spools. If they're a little loose, pack play dough around them to make them fit snugly.
- Set 9 marshmallows in a row on the cardboard and glue them into place. Glue the last marshmallow onto the one

in the center for the shammes. Insert the candles into the marshmallows.

- Make an edible menorah by using Ornamental Frosting to stick the marshmallows onto the cardboard. Use pretzel sticks instead of candles.
- Shape play dough into 9 Hanukkah designs or interesting shapes and insert the candles into the shapes.
- Fill a shoebox with sand and insert the candles into the sand. If you like, cover the outside of the box with paper and decorate it with Hanukkah designs.
- Drill 9 holes into a tree branch or driftwood and insert the candles into the holes.

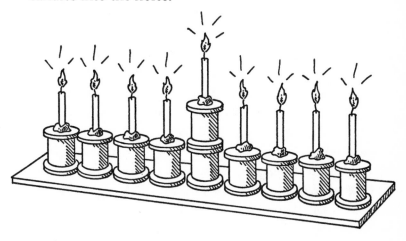

CHRISTMAS (DECEMBER 25)

Christmas is a time when Christians celebrate the birth of Jesus Christ. For some, Christmas means the arrival of Santa Claus, Father Christmas, Père Noël, or Saint Nicholas. Christmas celebrations usually emphasize family togetherness, thoughtful and loving acts, and good food.

But Christmas often brings more than peace, joy, love, and goodwill. For adults, Christmas can be frenzied, stressful, and financially demanding. Unrealistic expectations can make it hard to enjoy the season. Add too many late nights and too much rich food, and it's no wonder we breathe a sigh of relief when Christmas is over!

Make the most of your Christmas by forgetting what everyone else is doing and concentrating on what matters most to your family. Spend your time, money, and energy on activities that build or uphold family traditions and make memories for your child. Keep celebrations simple and stick to your child's regular meal and nap schedules so she gets the most out of the holiday. Use some of the drawing, painting, or other techniques described in previous chapters to create decorations and cards in Christmas colors. Read a book about Christmas, sing carols, bake cookies, and sip hot chocolate together. She'll soon forget toys and other things, but she'll never forget the memories you've made together.

Candy Advent Calendar

Ornamental Frosting (See Appendix A.)
Matte board, poster board, or heavy cardboard
Markers, stickers, rubber stamps, or scissors and used
  Christmas cards
Plastic knife
Wrapped Christmas candies
Hole punch
Ribbon

Make a batch of Ornamental Frosting. Draw an Advent calendar for your child on matte board, poster board, or heavy cardboard.

Have your child decorate her calendar with drawings, stickers, rubber stamps, or pictures cut from used Christmas cards. Let her use the plastic knife to spread the frosting on wrapped candies and stick one candy onto each space on the calendar. Lay the calendar flat until the frosting sets, then punch two holes in the top and loop ribbon through them for hanging.

Hang the calendar up and let your child remove a candy each day of Advent as a tasty reminder of the number of days until Christmas.

Ice Crystal Picture

Spoon
¼ cup water
½ cup Epsom salts, table salt, or rock salt
Small bowl
Crayons
Black, purple, or blue construction paper
Paintbrush
Clear contact paper (optional)
White chalk or tempera paint (optional)

Mix the water and salt in a small bowl. Stir to dissolve as much of the salt as possible. Have your child use the crayons to draw a nighttime forest scene on the paper. Include trees, stars, the moon, and an owl if she likes. Brush the drawing with the salt solution. Stir the solution each time you dip the brush in it to keep the brush saturated with salt water and to keep the solution well mixed. Let the painting dry completely. The salt will give a snowy, crystalline effect. The salt crystals will brush off the paper when it's dry, so cover it with clear contact paper if you like.

If you like, for a simple winter scene, draw with white chalk or paint with white tempera paint on dark blue or black construction paper.

Apple Centerpiece

Sharp knife
1 large apple
6-inch taper candle
Christmas greenery (holly, pine branches, and so on)

Slice the bottom off the apple so the top sits flat. Partially core the apple from the top so you have a hole as wide as the candle and about 2 inches deep. Insert the candle into the apple. Have your child poke the greenery into the apple to create a festive centerpiece. The greenery can dry out and become a fire hazard fairly quickly, so use caution if you light the candle.

Popcorn Snow

Paintbrush and white glue or glue stick
Dark-colored construction paper
Popped popcorn

Have your child brush or rub the glue on the paper. Then
have her stick popcorn onto the paper to make a winter scene.

Snow Pictures

Salt
Flour
Bowl
Empty saltshaker or spice container
Dark blue or black construction paper
Dishpan or cardboard box lid
Paintbrush
Water

Mix together equal parts of salt and flour in a bowl. Pour the
mixture into a saltshaker. Place the paper in the dishpan. Let
your child paint a design on the paper with water, then sprinkle
the salt/flour mixture on top to make a snowy picture.

Many Thanks

Most young children understand the concept of saying thank you, and sending thank-you notes for gifts they've received is a creative way for them to express their appreciation. With a little imagination you can help your child create one-of-a-kind thank-you notes.

- Before Christmas, take your child to a department store portrait studio and purchase an inexpensive package of photos, or have reprints made of an existing photo. Cut your child's face from the photo and glue it onto a frozen juice can lid. Have your child use a permanent marker to sign and date the back. Glue on a magnet, clasp, or ribbon loop and enclose the ornament in a thank-you note.
- Have your child use permanent markers to write a thank-you message on an inflated balloon that's not tied off. Deflate the balloon and send it in an envelope.
- Lay several Popsicle sticks side by side on a flat surface to form a square. Lay two pieces of tape across all the sticks to join them. Turn them over so the tape is on the under-side. Have your child write a thank-you message or draw or paint a picture on the Popsicle stick square. When the picture is complete, remove the tape to make a thank-you puzzle.

Sand Art Brownie Gift Mix

¾ *cup all-purpose flour*
1 teaspoon salt
1-quart canning jar with lid
½ *cup unsweetened cocoa powder*
¾ *cup all-purpose flour*
¾ *cup packed brown sugar*
¾ *cup granulated sugar*
½ *cup semisweet chocolate chips*
½ *cup white chocolate chips*
Scissors and Christmas fabric
Ribbon
Pen and decorative tag
½ *cup butterscotch or peanut butter chips (optional)*

1. Mix the flour with the salt in a small bowl. Help your child layer the ingredients in the jar, beginning with the flour/salt mixture, continuing in order, and ending with the white chocolate chips. (You may not need as many chips if there's little room left in the jar.) Screw on the lid.
2. Cut a circle of fabric about 4 inches wider than the diameter of the jar. Tie the fabric circle around the lid with ribbon.

3. Write the following directions on a decorative tag: "Sand Art Brownies: Combine the contents of the jar with 1 teaspoon vanilla, ¾ cup vegetable oil, and 4 eggs. Beat until just mixed. Pour into a greased 9-by-13-inch pan. Bake at 350°F for 25–30 minutes." Attach the tag to the jar.

If you like, substitute butterscotch or peanut butter chips for either of the chocolate chips.

Winter Windows

Liquid dish soap
White tempera paint
Paintbrush
Plastic wrap

Add a little dish soap to the paint. Have your child paint
designs or pictures on a window. Cover the windows with
plastic wrap and let the paint sit overnight. On the next day,
peel off the plastic wrap to see your frosty winter window.
The detergent will make the paint easily come off with
glass cleaner.

Greeting Card Chain

Scissors
Used Christmas cards
Stapler

Cut the cards to make horizontal strips. Show your child
how to loop one strip and staple the ends together. Insert a
second strip through the loop and staple its ends together to
form a second link on the chain. Continue this process until
the chain is as long as you like or until your child tires of
this project.

Candy Stocking

Red or green craft foam (or red or green construction paper
  covered with clear contact paper)
Clear plastic page protector
Scissors
Hole punch
Yarn or ribbon
Candy

Cut a stocking shape from the craft foam. Use the foam
cutout to cut a stocking shape from the page protector.
Holding the two cutouts together (plastic one on top), punch
holes all around the edges. Show your child how to lace yarn
or ribbon through the holes, beginning at a top corner of the
stocking and working down, around the toe, and up the other
side. Weave through each hole from front to back, and leave
about eight inches of yarn hanging from the first hole. Fill
the stocking with Christmas candy. Lace the opening shut
and tie the ends in a bow or a loop for hanging.

Sugar Cookie Bouquet

1 cup margarine
1½ cups sugar
2 eggs
1 teaspoon vanilla
3 cups flour
2 teaspoons baking powder
¼ teaspoon salt
1 cup powdered sugar
2 teaspoons milk
2 teaspoons light corn syrup
¼ teaspoon almond
  extract

Food coloring in holiday
  colors
Popsicle sticks
Plastic wrap or plastic
  sandwich bags
Florist's foam or Styrofoam
Decorated terra cotta pot
  (See page 271.)
Cellophane and ribbon
  (optional)

1. Preheat your oven to 350°F.
2. Combine the margarine and sugar in a large bowl.
3. Beat in the eggs one at a time, then add the vanilla.
4. Add the flour, baking powder, and salt. Stir until the mixture's blended.
5. Roll the dough into 2-inch balls. Place the balls on a baking sheet. Press down on each ball slightly, and insert a Popsicle stick into the top of each one. Leave space between the cookies as they will spread.
6. Bake the cookies 8–10 minutes or until they're golden brown. Let them cool.

7. In a small bowl, stir together the powdered sugar and milk until smooth. Beat in the corn syrup and almond extract until the frosting is smooth and glossy. If it's too thick, stir in more corn syrup. Divide the frosting into separate bowls. Add a different color of food coloring to each and mix well.

8. Have your child dip the cookies in frosting or paint it on with a new paintbrush.

9. Wrap each cookie individually with plastic wrap.

10. Insert florist's foam into the pot. Gently push the cookie pops into the foam. If you like, wrap the cookie bouquet with cellophane and a ribbon.

Christmas Prints

For this activity, be sure to use white craft glue, which leaves a raised line when it dries.

Pencil
Plain paper
White craft glue
Gold or silver paint

Brayer or paintbrush
Large sheet of tissue paper
  or newsprint
Clear contact paper (optional)

Lightly sketch some Christmas shapes on the paper. Have your child trace the outlines of the shapes with the craft glue. When the glue is dry, use a brayer or a paintbrush to paint gold or silver paint over the glue shapes. Before the paint dries, use the picture in one of the following ways:

- Fold a sheet of paper in half to make a card. Press the front of the card on the paint and rub gently to transfer the painted picture onto the card.
- Press the sheet of tissue paper or newsprint on the paint and rub gently. Lift the paper and press another section of the paper on the paint and rub again. Apply more paint as needed and continue rubbing the paper on the paint until the whole sheet is covered. Let the paint dry and use the sheet as gift-wrap.
- Press paper on the paint and rub gently. Add paint and repeat this process with more paper. Hang the pictures or cover them with the contact paper to make place mats.

Christmas Mobile

Pen or marker
Christmas cookie cutters
Construction paper
Scissors
Glitter pens or paint pens (optional)
Hole punch or tape
Dental floss or embroidery thread
Dinner-size paper plate (or file folder cut into a circle)

Trace around the cookie cutters on the paper and cut out the shapes. If you like, have your child decorate the shapes with glitter pens or paint pens. Punch a hole at the top of each shape (or use tape) to attach a floss or thread loop to each shape.

Beginning at one edge of the paper plate, cut along a spiral path, cutting around and around until you reach the center of the plate. Punch a hole in the center. Loop floss or thread through the hole. Punch as many holes as you have shapes at different places in the spiral, then tie a shape to each hole. Hang the mobile from the ceiling.

KWANZAA (DECEMBER 26–JANUARY 1)

Kwanzaa is a seven-day African-American cultural celebration. The Swahili word *kwanzaa* means "first fruit of the harvest," and the holiday is based on the traditional African winter harvest festival. During this time, African Americans reflect upon the year that's ending and celebrate their African heritage.

Kwanzaa begins the day after Christmas, but the two celebrations are very different. Kwanzaa celebrates the harvest and a way of life handed down by ancestors and parents. Special handmade gifts or educational games and books are exchanged, but Kwanzaa emphasizes values rather than gifts. Each day of the Kwanzaa week celebrates one of seven principles or values. These are unity, self-determination, collective work and responsibility, cooperative economics, purpose, creativity, and faith.

Even if your family isn't of African origin, you may enjoy doing a few simple Kwanzaa activities with your child. Try some of the ideas that follow or use some of the drawing, painting, printmaking, or other techniques described in previous chapters to create red, green, and black Kwanzaa decorations and gifts. Eat cornbread, peanut cookies, rice, or sweet potatoes. Learn more about Kwanzaa by reading a book like *My First Kwanzaa Book* by Deborah M. Newton Chocolate (Cartwheel Books, 1999).

Woven Mat

The woven mat, or *mkeka* (em-KAY-kah), is the mat on which the other Kwanzaa symbols rest. The mkeka is a symbol of tradition and history.

*Black, red, and green
    construction paper*

*Child's scissors
Glue or stapler*

Fold the black paper in half so the short edges meet. This will make a frame for the mat. Show your child how to cut from the folded edge to within 1 inch of the opposite side. Have her make seven cuts about 1-inch apart to make eight 1-inch sections. Unfold the paper. Cut 1-inch-wide strips from the red and green paper, cutting from long edge to long edge of each sheet. Show your child how to weave the strips over and under the cuts in the frame, alternating red and green strips. Glue or staple the strips in place along the edge of the frame. Trim the strips if necessary.

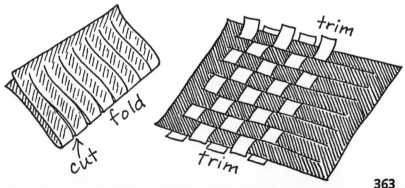

Kwanzaa Painting

Electric mixer, eggbeater, or wire whisk
1 cup grated Ivory soap (half a 4½-ounce bar)
½ cup cold water
Bowl
2 small containers
Red and green food coloring
Popsicle stick or paintbrush
Paper
Newspaper
Black construction paper or cardboard

Beat or whisk the soap and water together in a bowl until the mixture is stiff. Divide the mixture into the containers. Use food coloring to tint the mixture in one container red and the other green. Let your child paint with the soap paint in the one of the following ways:

- Use a Popsicle stick or paintbrush to spread the paint on paper.
- Use it as finger paint.
- Crumple up newspaper. Dip the newspaper into the paint, then press it onto the paper to make an interesting design.
- Completely cover black construction paper or cardboard with both colors of paint. Use a Popsicle stick, paintbrush, or your fingers to trace a design through the paint so the black paper shows through.

Corny Napkin Rings

Corn is a traditional part of the Kwanzaa celebration.

Scissors
Empty paper towel roll
Black, red, and/or green paint
White glue
Shallow containers
Paintbrush (optional)
Popcorn kernels

Cut the paper towel roll into 1-inch sections. In separate containers combine each color of paint with an equal amount of white glue. Have your child roll the outside of the rings in the colored glue, or brush it on with a paintbrush. Roll the rings in the popcorn kernels. When the glue is dry, insert a brightly colored napkin in the ring and use it in your Kwanzaa feast.

African Wildlife

Acrylic paint
Paintbrush
Animals crackers
Clear acrylic spray
Glue
Construction paper or
poster board

Paper clip
Ribbon or cord
Wooden picture frame
Magnets
Baking sheet

Have your child paint the animal crackers, and finish them with clear acrylic spray. Use the painted animals in one of the following ways:

- Glue them onto construction paper to create an African wildlife scene.
- Glue a paper clip onto the back of one of them. Thread ribbon through the paper clip to make a pendant necklace.
- Glue them onto a wooden picture frame.
- Glue small magnets onto their backs. Use them as refrigerator magnets or to act out scenes on a baking sheet.

Peanut Butter Sculptures

George Washington Carver was a famous African-American scientist who developed many uses for the peanut.

Peanut butter
Small plate or plastic container
Small plastic knife or Popsicle stick
Crackers
Cereal (optional)

Put the peanut butter on the plate. Have your child use the plastic knife or Popsicle stick to spread it onto a cracker, then stick another cracker on top of it. Let her continue building layers until her sculpture is complete. If you like, use a few different kinds of crackers and/or cereal.

Kwanzaa Cutouts

Scrap paper
Black, red, and green construction paper
Child's scissors
Glue

Use scrap paper to show your child how to cut out designs by folding the paper over and over and cutting shapes from the folds (geometric shapes like circles, squares, and triangles work well). Have your child fold the black paper and cut shapes from the folds. When her design is complete, show her how to cut pieces from the red and green paper to fit behind spaces in the black paper. Glue the pieces into place to create a colorful piece of art.

APPENDIX A
Basic Craft Recipes

Children begin to develop creative skills at a very early age. Most don't care as much about what they make as about the process of working with materials of many different colors and textures. Whether it's the process or the product that interests your child, the craft materials in this appendix are essential for his artwork. On the following pages you'll find easy recipes for paint, glue, paste, modeling compounds, and more.

PAINT

Each of the following recipes will produce a good-quality paint for your child's use. The ingredients and preparation vary from recipe to recipe, so choose one that best suits the supplies and time you have available.

When mixing paint, keep in mind the age of your young artist. As a general rule, younger children require thicker paint and brushes. Paint should always be stored in covered containers. Small plastic spillproof paint containers are available at art supply stores. Each comes with an airtight lid, holds brushes upright without tipping, and is well worth the purchase price of several dollars.

Condensed-Milk Paint

Bowl
1 cup condensed milk
Food coloring

In a bowl, mix the condensed milk with many drops of food coloring to make a very bright, glossy paint. This paint isn't intended to be eaten, but it won't harm a child who decides to snack on it. Store it covered in the refrigerator.

Flour-Based Poster Paint

¼ cup flour
Saucepan
1 cup water
Small jars or plastic containers
3 tablespoons powdered tempera
* paint per container*

2 tablespoons water per container
½ teaspoon liquid starch or liquid
* laundry detergent per container*
* (optional)*

Measure the flour into a saucepan. Slowly add 1 cup of water while stirring the mixture to make a smooth paste. Heat the paste, stirring constantly, until it begins to thicken. Let it cool. Measure ¼ cup of the paste into each container. Add 3 tablespoons of powdered tempera paint and 2 tablespoons of water to each container, using a different container for each color. If you like, add liquid starch for a matte finish or liquid laundry detergent for a glossy finish. Cover the containers for storage.

Cornstarch Paint

½ cup cornstarch
Medium saucepan
½ cup cold water
4 cups boiling water

Small jars or plastic containers
1 teaspoon powdered tempera
* paint or 1 tablespoon liquid*
* tempera paint per container*

Measure the cornstarch into the saucepan. Add the cold water and stir the mixture to make a smooth, thick paste. Stir in the boiling water. Place the saucepan over medium-low heat and stir the paste until it's boiling. Boil the paste for 1 minute, then remove it from the heat and let it cool. Spoon about ½ cup of the paste into each container. Stir 1 teaspoon of powdered tempera paint or 1 tablespoon of liquid tempera paint into each container, using a different container for each color. (Use more paint for a more intense color.) If the paint is too thick, stir in 1 teaspoon of water at a time until the desired consistency is achieved. Cover the containers and refrigerate them for storage.

Detergent Poster Paint

Small jars or plastic containers
1 tablespoon clear liquid laundry detergent per container
2 teaspoons powdered tempera paint per container

In each jar, mix 1 tablespoon of detergent and 2 teaspoons of powdered tempera paint. Use a different container for each color.

Edible Egg Yolk Paint

Small jars or plastic containers   *¼ teaspoon water per container*
1 egg yolk per container   *Food coloring*

In each jar, mix 1 egg yolk with ¼ teaspoon of water and many drops of food coloring. Use a paintbrush to apply paint to freshly baked cookies. Return cookies to the warm oven until the paint hardens.

Cornstarch Finger Paint

3 tablespoons sugar   *Muffin pan or small cups*
½ cup cornstarch   *Food coloring*
Medium saucepan   *Soap flakes or liquid dish soap*
2 cups cold water

Mix the sugar and cornstarch in the saucepan. Turn the heat on low, add the water, and stir the mixture constantly until it's thick. Remove it from the heat. Spoon the mixture into 4–5 muffin pan sections or small cups. Add a few drops of food coloring and a pinch of soap flakes or a drop of liquid dish soap to each cup. Stir the paint and let it cool before use. Cover the paint and refrigerate it for storage.

Flour Finger Paint

1 cup flour
2 tablespoons salt
Saucepan
1½ cups cold water

Wire whisk or eggbeater
1¼ cups hot water
Food coloring or powdered
  tempera paint

Mix the flour and salt in the saucepan. Beat in the cold water until the mixture is smooth. Mix in the hot water and boil the mixture until it's thick, then beat it again until it's smooth. Tint the paint however you like with food coloring or powdered tempera paint. Cover the paint and refrigerate it for storage.

Milk Paint

2 tablespoons nonfat dry milk
Small bowl

Warm water
Food coloring

Measure the dry milk into the bowl. Add enough warm water to make a thick paste. Add a few drops of food coloring and stir the mixture until it's smooth. Cover the paint and refrigerate it for storage.

Corn Syrup Paint

4 tablespoons corn syrup
1½ teaspoons liquid dish soap
Small container
Liquid tempera paint or food coloring

Mix the corn syrup and dish soap in the container. Add enough liquid tempera paint or food coloring to color the paint. Use a different container for each color.

Puffy Paint

Flour
Salt
Water
Bowl

Food coloring or liquid tempera
*   paint (optional)*
Squeeze bottles

Mix equal parts of the flour, salt, and water in a bowl. If you like, add food coloring or liquid tempera paint to color the paint. Pour the paint into squeeze bottles.

Crystal Paint

1 cup Epsom salts
½ cup water
Bowl

Small containers or Styrofoam
*   egg carton*
Food coloring or liquid tempera
*   paint*

Combine the salts and water in a bowl. Pour the mixture into the containers. Add a few drops of food coloring or liquid tempera paint to each container, a different color for each. Mix the paint well.

Fluffy Soap Paint

Electric mixer, eggbeater, or
*   wire whisk*
1 cup grated Ivory soap
*   (half a 4½ ounce bar)*

½ cup cold water
Bowl
Food coloring (optional)

Beat or whisk the soap and water together in a bowl until the mixture is stiff and thick. If you like, add food coloring to tint the paint.

PLAY DOUGH

Each of the following recipes produces a good-quality play dough. Some require cooking and some don't. Choose the recipe that best suits your needs and the ingredients you have on hand. Store play dough in a covered container or Ziploc bag. If it sweats a little, just add more flour. For sensory variety, warm or chill play dough before using.

Oatmeal Play Dough

Your child will be able to make this play dough with little help, but it doesn't last as long as cooked play dough. This play dough isn't meant to be eaten, but it won't hurt a child who decides to taste it.

1 part flour　　　　　　　　　*2 parts oatmeal*
1 part water　　　　　　　　　*Bowl*

Place all the ingredients in a bowl. Mix them well and knead the dough until it's smooth. Cover the play dough and refrigerate it for storage.

Uncooked Play Dough

Bowl　　　　　　　　　　　*Tempera paint or food coloring*
1 cup cold water　　　　　　*3 cups flour*
1 cup salt　　　　　　　　　*2 tablespoons cornstarch*
2 teaspoons vegetable oil

In a bowl, mix the water, salt, oil, and enough tempera paint or food coloring to make a brightly colored mixture. Gradually blend in the flour and cornstarch until the mixture has the consistency of bread dough. Cover the play dough for storage.

Salt Play Dough

1 cup salt
1 cup water

½ cup plus more flour
Saucepan

Mix the salt, water, and ½ cup of flour in a saucepan. Stir and cook the mixture over medium heat. Remove it from the heat when it's thick and rubbery. As the mixture cools, knead in enough additional flour to make the dough workable.

Colored Play Dough

Cream of tartar makes this play dough last 6 months or longer, so resist the temptation to omit this ingredient if you don't have it on hand.

1 cup water
1 tablespoon vegetable oil
½ cup salt
1 tablespoon cream of tartar

Food coloring
Saucepan
1 cup flour

Mix the water, oil, salt, cream of tartar, and a few drops of food coloring in a saucepan and heat the mixture until it's warm. Remove the mixture from the heat and stir in the flour. Knead the dough until it's smooth.

Kool-Aid Play Dough

This dough will last 2 months or longer.

½ cup salt
2 cups water
Saucepan
Kool-Aid mix, food coloring, or
*   powdered tempera paint*

2 tablespoons vegetable oil
2 cups sifted flour
2 tablespoons alum

Mix the salt and water in a saucepan and boil the mixture until the salt dissolves. Remove the mixture from the heat and tint it with Kool-Aid mix, food coloring, or powdered tempera paint. Add the oil, flour, and alum. Knead the dough until it's smooth.

CLAY

Use the following recipes to make clay that can be rolled or shaped into sculptures. Some clays should be dried overnight, while others are best baked in an oven. When hard, sculptures can be decorated with paint, markers, and/or glitter and preserved with shellac, acrylic spray, or clear nail polish. Store leftover clay in a covered container or Ziploc bag. Please note that none of these clays is edible.

Modeling Clay

2 cups salt
⅔ cup water
Saucepan

1 cup cornstarch
½ cup cold water

Stir the salt and ⅔ cup of water in a saucepan over heat for 4–5 minutes. Remove the mixture from the heat. Blend in the cornstarch and cold water until the mixture is smooth. Return it to the heat and cook it until it's thick. Let the clay cool, then shape it however you like. Let your sculpture dry overnight before decorating and finishing it.

Baker's Clay

4 cups flour
1 cup salt
1 teaspoon alum
1½ cups water
Large bowl

Food coloring (optional)
*Rolling pin, cookie cutters, drinking
    straw, and fine wire (optional)*
Baking sheet
Fine sandpaper

Preheat your oven to 250°F. Mix the flour, salt, alum, and water in a large bowl. If the clay is too dry, knead in another tablespoon of water. If you like, tint the clay by dividing it and kneading a few drops of food coloring into each portion. Shape the clay however you like. To make hanging ornaments, roll or mold the clay as follows, then attach a loop of fine wire to each ornament.

- **To roll:** Roll the clay ⅛ inch thick on a lightly floured surface. Cut it with cookie cutters dipped in flour. Make a hole for hanging the ornament by dipping the end of a drinking straw in flour and using the straw to cut a tiny hole ¼ inch from the ornament's edge. You can also use the straw to cut more clay dots for press-on decorations.
- **To mold:** Shape the clay into flowers, fruits, animals, and so on. The figures should be no more than ½ inch thick.

Bake your sculpture(s) on an ungreased baking sheet for about 30 minutes. Turn and bake them for another 90 minutes until they're hard and dry. Remove them from the oven and let them cool, then smooth them with fine sandpaper before decorating and finishing them.

No-Bake Craft Clay

Food coloring (optional)
1¼ cups cold water
1 cup cornstarch
2 cups baking soda

Saucepan
Plate
Damp cloth

If you want tinted clay, mix a few drops of food coloring into the water. Then mix the water, cornstarch, and baking soda in a saucepan over medium heat for about 4 minutes until the mixture has the consistency of moist mashed potatoes. Remove the mixture from the heat, turn it onto a plate, and cover it with a damp cloth until it's cool. Knead the clay until it's smooth, then shape it however you like. Let your sculpture dry overnight before decorating and finishing it.

Salt Clay

1 cup flour
½ cup salt
Water

Bowl
Food coloring (optional)

Mix the flour and salt with enough water in a bowl to make a dough that feels like modeling clay. If you like, tint the dough with food coloring. This dough can be shaped and rolled, then baked at 200°F for 1–2 hours until hard.

GLUE AND PASTE

The following recipes use a variety of ingredients, and the resulting glues and pastes have a variety of uses. Choose the one that best suits your project. For fun, add food coloring to glue or paste before using it. Store all glues and pastes in airtight containers in the refrigerator.

Glue

2 tablespoons corn syrup
1 teaspoon white vinegar
¾ cup water
Small saucepan

Small bowl
2 tablespoons cornstarch
¾ cup cold water

Mix the corn syrup, vinegar, and ¾ cup of water in a small saucepan. Bring the mixture to a full rolling boil. In a small bowl, mix the cornstarch and cold water. Stir this mixture slowly into the hot mixture until it begins to boil again. Boil the mixture for 1 minute, then remove it from the heat. When it's cooled slightly, pour it into another container and let it stand overnight before you use it.

Homemade Paste

This wet, messy paste takes a while to dry.

½ cup flour   *Cold water*
Saucepan

Measure the flour into a saucepan. Stir in cold water until the mixture is as thick as cream. Simmer the mixture, stirring constantly, for 5 minutes. Remove it from the heat and let it cool before you use it.

Papier-Mâché Paste

6 cups water   *¼ cup flour*
Saucepan   *Small bowl*

Lightly boil 5 cups of water in a saucepan. Measure the flour into a small bowl. Stir in 1 cup of water to make a runny mixture. Stir this mixture into the boiling water. Stir and gently boil the paste for 2–3 minutes. Let it cool before you use it.

No-Cook Paste

½ cup flour
Water
Salt

Mix the flour and water until the mixture is gooey. Stir in a pinch of salt.

OTHER CRAFT RECIPES

Use the following recipes to make interesting supplies for various arts and crafts projects.

Colorful Creative Salt

Use this salt as you would use glitter.

Small bowl
5–6 drops food coloring

½ cup salt
Microwave or wax paper

In a small bowl, stir the food coloring into the salt. Microwave the mixture for 1–2 minutes or spread it on wax paper and let it air-dry. Store the salt in an airtight container.

Dyed Pasta

½ cup rubbing alcohol
Food coloring
Small bowl

Dry pasta
Newspaper and wax paper

Mix the alcohol and food coloring in a small bowl. Add small amounts of dry pasta to the liquid and mix it gently. The larger the pasta, the longer it will take to absorb the color. Dry the dyed pasta on newspaper covered with wax paper.

Ornamental Frosting

This frosting is an edible glue. Use it for gingerbread houses or other food art. It can be made several hours or a day before you use it.

Electric mixer or eggbeater
3 egg whites
1 teaspoon cream of tartar

Bowl
4 cups powdered sugar
Damp cloth

Beat the egg whites and cream of tartar in a bowl until stiff peaks form. Add the powdered sugar and continue beating the frosting until it's thick and holds its shape. Cover the frosting with a damp cloth when you're not using it. Store it in an airtight container in the refrigerator.

Homemade Chalk

Toilet paper or paper towel tubes
Scissors
Duct tape
Wax paper
¾ cup warm water

Small bucket or disposable
*   container*
1½ cups plaster of Paris
2–3 tablespoons powdered
*   tempera paint*

If using paper towel tubes, cut each tube in half. Cover one end of each paper tube with duct tape. Cut as many pieces of wax paper as you have tubes. Each piece should be as long as the tube and about 4 inches wide. Roll up each piece of wax paper and slip it into a tube.

Pour the water into the bucket. Sprinkle the plaster of Paris over the water and stir the mixture thoroughly with a spoon. Mix in the tempera paint.

Place each tube tape side down on a level surface. Pour the wet plaster mixture into the tubes. Lightly tap the sides of each tube to release air bubbles, then set the plaster-filled tube aside to harden for a few days. Peel off the tubes and wax paper to use the chalk.

APPENDIX B
Making Books with Children

Creating books with your child is fun to do and can be as simple or complex as you wish. Some home-schoolers spend weeks creating professional-looking bound books, but the process needn't be time-consuming. If you like, you can simply staple sheets of paper inside a construction paper cover or use a small notebook, scrapbook, photo album, or three-ring binder with plastic page protectors. Print the story your child dictates at the bottom of each page, then let your child illustrate the pages with his own artwork, photos, or pictures cut from magazines.

Making a bound book with your child takes a little more time, but the quality of the finished book makes it well worth the effort. The following instructions were adapted from the book *Parents Are Teachers, Too* by Claudia Jones (Williamson Publishing Co., 1988).

Scissors
1 sheet construction paper
Up to 8 sheets plain white paper
  (8½-by-11 inches)
Sewing machine or needle and
  thread
Utility knife (optional)

Cardboard or matte board
Nonstretch fabric
Paintbrush
White glue thinned with water
Wax paper
Several heavy books

1. Cut the construction paper to 8½-by-11 inches. Stack up to 8 sheets of plain paper on top of the construction paper. Fold the whole stack in half, with the construction paper on the outside. Stitch along the fold with a sewing machine or needle and thread.

2. Use a utility knife or scissors to cut 2 pieces of cardboard or matte board each measuring 5½-by-6¾ inches. Lay the 2 pieces side by side about ¼ inch apart on the wrong side of a piece of non-stretch fabric. Trim the fabric, leaving a 1-inch border on all sides of the cardboard or matte board.

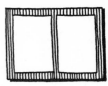

3. Paint a layer of watery white glue on one side of each piece of cardboard or matte board. Place the pieces of cardboard or matte board back in position (glue side down) on the fabric and press on them to glue them to the fabric.

4. Brush glue on the 1-inch fabric border, then fold the fabric over onto the cardboard. Smooth out the edges of the fabric as best you can, but don't worry about them too much, as they will be covered up in the next step.

5. Open the paper booklet you made in step 1. Paint the entire outside surface of the construction paper cover with glue. Press the gluey construction paper onto the inside of the fabric-covered cardboard cover.

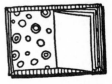

6. Place wax paper inside the front and back covers. Close the book and place more wax paper around the outside of the book. Then place it under a stack of heavy books so it will dry flat.

Illustrations for Appendix B by Terri Moll

APPENDIX C
Books for Children

Arts and crafts projects help children learn and/or develop cooperation skills, expression of feelings, aesthetic appreciation, motor control, reading readiness, vocabulary, flexible thinking, and basic math skills. Enhance your child's development of these skills by having him look at and talk about art, and by reading books about colors, shapes, patterns, and so on, like those listed below.

Some of these books are out of print and unavailable to purchase new, but you should be able to borrow all of them from your local library.

Bang, Molly
  Yellow Ball

Brown, Marcia
  Listen to a Shape
  Touch Will Tell
  Walk with Your Eyes

Brown, Margaret Wise
  Big Red Barn

Bruna, Dick
  My Shirt Is White

Carle, Eric
  My Very First Book of Colors

Crews, Donald
  Freight Train
  Parade

Demarest, Chris L.
  My Blue Boat

Emberley, Ed
  Green Says Go

Florian, Douglas
  A Carpenter

Grossman, Barney and Gladys Groom
  Black Means ...

Hamanaka, Sheila
  All the Colors of the Earth

Hoban, Tana
  Circles, Triangles, and Squares
  Colors Everywhere
  Is It Red? Is It Yellow? Is It Blue?
  Shapes and Things

Hughes, Shirley
  All Shapes and Sizes

Hutchins, Pat
  Little Pink Pig

Johnson, Crockett
  Harold and the Purple Crayon

Lionni, Leo
  Little Blue and Little Yellow

Martin, Bill Jr. and Eric Carle
  *Brown Bear, Brown Bear, What
  Do You See?*

McGovern, Ann
  Black Is Beautiful

McMillan, Bruce
  Growing Colors

Miles, Miska
  Apricot ABC

Miller, Margaret
  My Five Senses

Munsch, Robert
  Purple, Green and Yellow

O'Neill, Mary
  Hailstones and Halibut Bones

Patilla, Peter
  Starting off with Shapes

Pienkowski, Jan
  Colors
  Shapes

Reiss, John J.
  Colors
  Shapes

Showers, Paul
  Find Out by Touching

Stocks, Sue
  Collage

Tester, Sylvia Root
  A World of Color

Tresselt, Alvin
  White Snow, Bright Snow

Winter, Jonah
  Frida

Woolfitt, Gabrielle
  Blue
  Green
  Red
  Yellow

APPENDIX D
Resources for Parents

In writing this book I gleaned ideas and information from personal experience, friends and family, and the books listed below.

Bawden, Juliet. *101 Things to Make.* New York: Sterling Publishing Co., 1994.

Cohen, Cambria. *50 Nifty Super Crafts to Make with Things Around the House.* Los Angeles: Lowell House Juvenile, 1999.

Cook, Deanna F., ed. *Disney's FamilyFun Crafts.* New York: Hyperion, 1997.

Dahlstrom, Carol Field, ed. *More Incredibly Awesome Crafts for Kids.* Des Moines: Better Homes and Gardens Books, 1997.

Deshpande, Chris. *Food Crafts.* Milwaukee, Wis.: Gareth Stevens Publishing, 1994.

Erickson, Donna. *Prime Time Together...With Kids.* Minneapolis: Augsburg Fortress, 1989.

Gibson, Ray. *The Usborne Book of Papier Mâché.* London: Usborne Publishing, 1995.

Hamilton, Leslie. *Child's Play.* New York: Crown Publishers, 1992.

Hauser, Jill Frankel. *Easy Art Fun!* Charlotte, Vt.: Williamson Publishing Co., 2002.

Jones, Claudia. *Parents Are Teachers, Too.* Charlotte, Vt: Williamson Publishing Co., 1988.

Kohl, MaryAnn F. and Jean Potter. *Cooking Art.* Beltsville, Md.: Gryphon Publishing House, 1997.

Kohl, MaryAnn F. *Preschool Art.* Beltsville, Md.: Gryphon Publishing House, 1994.

Kuffner, Trish. *The Children's Busy Book*. Minnetonka, Minn.: Meadowbrook Press, 2001.

Kuffner, Trish. *Picture Book Activities*. Minnetonka, Minn.: Meadowbrook Press, 2001.

Kuffner, Trish. *The Preschooler's Busy Book*. Minnetonka, Minn.: Meadowbrook Press, 1998.

Kuffner, Trish. *The Toddler's Busy Book,* Minnetonka, Minn.: Meadowbrook Press, 1999.

Lacey, Sue. *Art for Fun Projects*. Brookfield, Conn.: Millbrook Press, 2001.

Mackenzie, Jennie. *Creative Fun Crafts for Kids*. Menlo Park, Calif.: Sunset Publishing, 1993.

MacLeod, Elizabeth. *Bake It and Build It*. Toronto: Kids Can Press, 1998.

Mayesky, Mary. *Creative Activities for Young Children,* 4th Edition. Albany, N.Y.: Delmar Publishers Inc., 1990.

Miller, Karen. *More Things to Do with Toddlers and Twos*. Chelsea, Mass.: Telshare Publishing Co. Ltd., 1990.

Milord, Susan. *Adventures in Art*. Charlotte, Vt.: Williamson Publishing, 1990.

Morris, Eileen and Stephanie Pereau Crilly. *Get Ready, Set, Grow!* Belmont, Calif.: Fearon (David S. Lake Publishers), 1984.

Polonsky, Lydia et al. *Math for the Very Young*. New York: John Wiley & Sons, 1995.

Press, Judy. *ArtStarts for Little Hands!* Charlotte, Vt.: Williamson Publishing, 2000.

Robins, Deri. *Papier-Mâché*. New York: Kingfisher Books, 1993.

Ross, Kathy. *Crafts to Make in the Winter*. Brookfield, Conn.: Millbrook Press, 1999.

Ross, Kathy. *Crafts for Kids Who Are Wild About the Wild.* Brookfield, Conn.: Millbrook Press, 1998.

Ross, Kathy. *Gifts to Make for Your Favorite Grownup.* Brookfield, Conn.: Millbrook Press, 1996.

Sadler, Judy Ann. *The Kids Can Press Jumbo Book of Easy Crafts.* Toronto: Kids Can Press, 2001.

Sanford, Anne R. *A Planning Guide to the Preschool Curriculum.* Winston-Salem, N.C.: Kaplan Press, 1983.

Swain, Gwenyth, *Bookworks.* Minneapolis: Carolrhoda Books, 1995.

Umnik, Sharon Dunn, ed. *175 Easy-to-Do Everyday Crafts.* Honesdale, Pa.: Boyds Mills Press, 1995.

Watt, Fiona. *Usborne Book of Art Ideas.* New York: Scholastic, 1999.

Wirtenberg, Patricia Z. *All-Around-the-House Art and Craft Book.* Boston: Houghton Mifflin, 1968.

Index

A

African Wildlife, 366
Alphabet Book, 249
Alphabet Cookies, 190
Alphabet Crackers, 207
Alphabet Prints, 93
Animal Snacks, 215
Apple Centerpiece, 351
Art Book, 161
Arts and Crafts for Toddlers, 9
Arty Apparel, 261
Autumn Colors Collage, 333

B

Ball Painting, 73
Balloon Art, 41
Basic Craft Recipes, 369
Bathtub Paint, 59
Beaded Coaster, 267
Beastly Bats, 328
Beautiful Butterfly, 272
Berry Ink, 178
Bird Buffet, 179
Bird's Nest Snack, 310
Biscuit Shapes, 223
Black Cat, 327
Bleach Pictures, 38
Bleached Leaf Prints, 186
Blob Painting, 67

Body Tracing, 21
Books for Children, 384
Bread Clay Sculptures, 105
Bread Sculptures, 212
Broom Painting, 78
Budding Illustrator, 24
Bungee Prints, 90
Burlap Prints, 334
Button Board, 230
Button Collage, 233
Button Necklace, 260
Button Prints, 96

C

Calendar Math, 240
Canada Day, 313
Candle Art, 275
Candy Advent Calendar, 349
Candy Jar, 274
Candy Sculptures, 222
Candy Stocking, 357
Cappuccino Gift Mix, 277
Cardboard Construction, 108
CD Picture Frame, 281
Chalk Fun, 26
Chalk Prints, 82
Charm Bracelet, 160
Chocolate Chip Cookie Cake, 216
Chocolate Spiders, 329
Christmas, 348

Christmas Mobile, 361
Christmas Prints, 360
Cinnamon-Applesauce Ornaments, 100
Circle Animal, 145
Clay, 376
Clay Beads, 120
Clay Magnets, 119
Clay Mosaic, 273
Clay Pot, 122
Clay Tablets, 121
Coffee Filter Art, 39
Coin Bank, 267
Color Collage, 244
Colored Photos, 41
Colorful Cookies, 209
Colorful Cubes, 221
Comb Painting, 72
Consumable Collage, 224
Cookie Cutter Ornaments, 101
Cookie Hamburgers, 323
Corncob Prints, 92
Cornucopia Place Cards, 338
Corny Napkin Rings, 365
Crayon Basics, 17
Crayon Design, 30
Crayon Engraving, 34
Crayon Prints, 91
Crazy Crayons, 15
Create-a-Color, 57
Creature Racers, 256

Crispy Rice Treats, 204
Crumpled Paper Painting, 51
Crystal Painting, 65
Cup of Cocoa, 276
Cutting Practice, 142

D

Dabber Painting, 48
Decorated Shoelaces, 256
Decoupage Basket, 158
Dipping Designs, 62
Dots and Lines, 25
Dough Play, 118
Drawing Challenge, 19
Dreidel, 342
Dribble Art, 37
Dried Flowers, 177

E

Easel Art, 16
Easter, 304
Easy Egg Mosaic, 305
Easy Embroidery, 268
Easy Fabric Wreath, 283
Edible Edifice, 211
Edible Mud Shapes, 192
Edible Pattern, 236
Edible Shapes, 219
Egg Decorating, 306
Egg Roll Art, 307

Eggs in the Grass, 312
Envelopes, 152
Eraser Art, 25
Eraser Block Prints, 85

F

Fabric Batik, 280
Fabric Collage, 148
Fabric Transfers, 33
Family Collage, 144
Family Phone Book, 248
Faux Gilding, 75
Finger Gelatin Fun, 198
Finger Painting, 58
Fireworks Painting, 316
First Words Scrapbook, 243
Flag Fun, 314
Flower Crown, 165
Flower Press, 175
Foil Engraving, 35
Food Collage, 143
Food Coloring Fun, 52
Four Seasons Poster, 239
Fourth of July Noisemakers, 319
Fourth of July Window Hanging, 324
Froot Loop Art, 140
Fruit and Vegetable Prints, 95
Fruit Shapes, 193
Funny Feet, 77
Funny Friend, 141
Fuzzy Chick Picture, 311

G

Gift Bag, 155
Gingerbread Critters, 208
Glue and Paste, 378
Glue Design, 74
Graham Cracker Gift Box, 218
Grape Surprise, 193
Green Collage, 300
Greeting Card Chain, 356

H

Halloween, 325
Handy Memories, 260
Hanukkah, 339
Hanukkah Cookies, 344
Hanukkah Mosaic, 345
Hanukkah Shapes, 340
Hidden Messages, 292
Homemade Stationery, 151
Hot Cross Buns, 308

I

"I Can" Scrapbook, 246
Ice Cream Cone Clowns, 195
Ice Cream Paint, 321
Ice Crystal Picture, 350
Ice Ornament, 184
Ice Painting, 56
Independence Day, 318
Introduction, vii
Irish Toast, 303

J

Jellybean Picture, 199

K

Keepsake Book, 257
Kwanzaa, 362
Kwanzaa Cutouts, 368
Kwanzaa Painting, 364

L

Lantern Garland, 149
Layered Sand Art, 266
Leaf Art, 173
Leaf Print Note Cards, 178
Leaf Stenciling, 174
Letter Puzzles, 246
Lollipop Treats, 326

M

Magical Mystery Mud, 106
Magnet Painting, 73
Magnetic Sign, 263
Making Books with Children, 382
Many Thanks, 353
Map Skills, 242
Maple Leaf Place Mats, 315
Maple Leaf Snacks, 316
Marker Play, 18
Marshmallow Shapes, 107
Melted-Crayon Drawing, 31

Menorah, 346
Michelangelo Painting, 67
Milk Paint, 75
Mirror Painting, 68
Molded Ornaments, 99
Mosaic Art, 150
Moss Wreath, 269
Mud Play, 172
Mud Puddle Painting, 170
Musical Instruments, 254
My Day Poster, 22

N

Natural Dye, 183
Nature Bookmark, 176
Nature Collage, 168
Nature Collection, 167
Nature Colors, 187
Nature Painting, 169
Necktie Snake, 282
Negative Painting, 69
Negative Plaster Imprints, 116
Nest Depot, 180
Newspaper Fruit, 133
Newspaper Platter, 134
Nibbly Necklace, 202
Nighttime Painting, 65
No-Bake Clay Sculptures, 105
No-Sew Cape, 279
Number Book, 234
Number Cards, 235

O

Object Prints, 81
Old Glory Tablecloth, 320
One Last Thought, 12
Organizing and Planning for Arts
  and Crafts, 2
Other Craft Recipes, 379

P

Paddy's Day Paint, 299
Paint, 369
Paint Pens, 27
Paint Prints, 86
Paint Roller Prints, 83
Painted Cookies, 200
Painted Eggs, 210
Painted Pebbles, 182
Painted Pot, 271
Painted Sticks, 238
Painted Tile, 264
Painting Fun, 47
Paper Batik, 32
Paper Beads, 159
Paper Border, 153
Paper Chain, 156
Papier-Mâché Beads, 123
Papier-Mâché Bowl, 124
Papier-Mâché Creation, 129
Papier-Mâché Finger Puppets, 128
Papier-Mâché Fish Piñata, 126
Papier-Mâché Napkin Rings, 125

Papier-Mâché Piggy Bank, 132
Papier-Mâché Pulp, 127
Papier-Mâché Pulp Objects, 130
Party Favors, 285
Pasta Sculptures, 114
Pastry Cookies, 206
Pattern Play, 237
Peanut Butter Logs, 213
Peanut Butter Play Dough, 197
Peanut Butter Pudding Paint, 196
Peanut Butter Sculptures, 367
Personal Record Book, 250
Personal Time Line, 247
Photo Puzzle, 155
Picnic Collage, 317
Pinless Bulletin Board, 270
Plaster Nature Art, 188
Play Dough, 374
Play Dough Balls, 117
Play Dough Shapes, 232
Popcorn Animals, 194
Popcorn Pumpkins, 336
Popcorn Snow, 352
Positive Plaster Imprints, 115
Poster Child, 20
Potato Sculptures, 219
Potpourri Air Freshener, 274
Powdered Paint, 53
Pretzels, 214
Printed Place Mat, 90
Printing Fun, 80
Printing Press, 87
Puffed Wheat Kisses, 295

Puffed Wheat Treats, 220
Puffy Painting, 54
Pumpkin Drawing, 329
Pumpkin Finger Paint, 336
Pumpkin Math, 331
Punch-Out Shamrock, 302
Putty Play, 118

R

Rainbow Painting, 76
Rainbow Paper Chain, 154
Raisin Play, 244
Ready to Read, 245
Red-and-White Painting, 315
Red, White, and Blue Cake, 322
Resources for Parents, 386
Rice Art, 139
Rock Painting, 170
Roller Painting, 61

S

Saint Patrick's Day, 296
Salt Art, 137
Salt Painting, 74
Sand Art Brownie Gift Mix, 354
Sandcasting, 113
Sandpaper Prints, 94
Scented Paint, 51
Scented Shamrock, 297
Scissors Fun, 140
Scouring Pad Prints, 82

Scrap Art, 138
See-Through Art, 39
Seed Count, 233
Seedy Sponge, 185
Shake Painting, 50
Shamrock Magnet, 298
Shamrock Prints, 301
Shape Collage, 142
Shape Painting, 227
Shell Painting, 182
Shiny Paint, 66
Shiny Shapes, 226
Shortbread Valentine Cookies, 294
Silhouette Portrait, 23
Snail Shells, 205
Snow Art, 171
Snow Pictures, 352
Snow Sculptures, 109
Soap Clay, 104
Soap Fluff, 102
Soap Mush, 104
Soap Powder Pictures, 42
Soda Can Prints, 88
Spaghetti Painting, 78
Spatter Painting, 70
Spice Pictures, 139
Spice Turkey, 335
Spiced Tea Treat, 278
Spider Crackers, 203
Spider Web, 330
Sponge Prints, 89
Spray Painting, 64
Squashed Painting, 60

Squish Squash, 103
Squishy Paint, 49
Star of David, 341
Stencil Hearts, 291
Stick Puppets, 258
Sticky Collage, 146
Sticky Dot Collage, 147
Stocking Up on Supplies, 5
String Art, 162
String Prints, 84
Stringing Straw, 265
Striped Painting, 71
Stuffed Hearts, 290
Styrofoam Structures, 110
Sugar Cookie Bouquet, 358
Sugar Cube Mosaic, 111
Sugar Cube Shapes, 112
Sugar Drawing, 40
Sun Painting, 185
Swat Painting, 55
Syrup Paint, 63

T

Table Rubbings, 252
Tactile Letters, 229
Telling Time, 241
Texture Rubbings, 29
Textured Painting, 71
Textured Prints, 96
Thanksgiving, 332
Thanksgiving Thankfulness, 337
Thirsty Celery, 166

3-D Nature Collage, 164
3-D Number Board, 231
Thumbprint Flowers, 36
Tie-Dyed Socks, 259
Tipped Painting, 76
Tissue Paper Prints, 85
Tracing Collage, 228
Triangle Fun, 230
T-Shirt Art, 284
Twig Frame, 181

V

Valentine Bookmarks, 292
Valentine Place Cards, 293
Valentine's Day, 289
Voilà! What Now?, 11

W

Water Painting, 50
Wax Resist Rubbings, 28
Weaving Wall, 187
Whipped Cream Finger Paint, 63
Winter Windows, 356
Woven Mat, 363

Z

Zigzag Strips, 159
Zipper Bracelets, 262
Zoo Sandwiches, 215

Also from Meadowbrook Press

✦ **Busy Books**
The Children's Busy Book, The Toddler's Busy Book, and *The Preschooler's Busy Book* each contains 365 activities (one for each day of the year) for your children using items found around the home. The books offer parents and child-care providers fun reading, math, and science activities that will stimulate a child's natural curiosity. They also provide great activities for indoor play during even the longest stretches of bad weather! All three books show you how to save money by making your own paints, play dough, craft clays, glue, paste, and other arts and crafts supplies.

✦ **Quality Time Anytime**
Over 200 games and activities to help parents and their children turn moments spent in the car, kitchen, bath, bedroom, outdoors, store—in short, anytime—into quality time! Enhance that special bond with your child, and teach social skills that will prove valuable the rest of your child's life.

✦ **Discipline without Shouting or Spanking**
The most practical guide to discipline available, this newly revised book provides proven methods for handling the 30 most common forms of childhood misbehavior, from temper tantrums to sibling rivalry.

**We offer many more titles written to delight, inform, and entertain.
To order books with a credit card or browse our full
selection of titles, visit our web site at:**

www.meadowbrookpress.com

or call toll-free to place an order, request a free catalog, or ask a question:

1-800-338-2232

Meadowbrook Press • 5451 Smetana Drive • Minnetonka, MN • 55343